What Zizi Gave Honeyboy

WILLIAM MORROW

An Imprint of HarperCollins*Publishers*

What Zizi Gave Honeyboy

A True Story About
Love, Wisdom, and
the Soul of America

Gerald Celente

Founder/Director of the Trends Research Institute

Grateful acknowledgment is made for permission to reprint from the following:

"Sonny Boy" by B. G. DeSylva, Lew Brown, Ray Henderson, and Al Jolson copyright © 1928 (renewed) by DeSylva, Brown & Henderson, Inc. Rights for extended renewal term in U.S. controlled by Chappell & Co., Ray Henderson Music Company, and Stephen Ballentine Music. Rights for Canada controlled by Chappell & Co. All rights reserved. Used by permission. Warner Bros. Publications U.S. Inc., Miami, Florida, 33014. "Forgive Me" by Jack Yellen and Milton Ager copyright © 1927 (renewed) Warner Bros. Inc. All rights reserved. Used by permission. Warner Bros. Publications U.S. Inc., Miami, FL 33014.

"Compassion" on page 199 and "Emperor Angel" on page 204 by Marie-Pierre Astier.

HarperCollins books may be purchased for educational, business, or sales promotional use. For information please write: Special Markets Department, HarperCollins Publishers Inc., 10 East 53rd Street, New York, NY 10022.

FIRST EDITION

Designed by Claire Vaccaro

All photographs courtesy of the author.

Printed on acid-free paper

Library of Congress Cataloging-in-Publication Data
Celente, Gerald, 1946–
What Zizi gave Honeyboy : a true story about love, wisdom, and
the soul of America / Gerald Celente.
p. cm.
ISBN 0-06-621266-9
1. Italian American women—Biography.   2. Aunts—United States—Biography.
3. Celente, Gerald, 1946–   4. Italian Americans—Biography.   5. Nephews—
United States—Biography.   6. Italian American families—Biography.   7. Social
values—United States.   8. United States—Social conditions—1945–
9. Yonkers (N.Y.)—Biography.   I. Title.
E184.I8 C39   2002
305.85'1073'092—dc21
[B]   2001044053

02   03   04   05   06   QW   10   9   8   7   6   5   4   3   2   1

Dedication

To all the departed souls who gave me so much love

and joy, and for the blessing of being the child of

Louis and Marie

Contents

Contents

A Note from the Author

Through the years, at the kitchen table of her little house in Yonkers, New York, Zizi has pampered me with her special blend of food, faith, friendship, and motherly love. But something different began to happen during my visits in the spring of 1999. Suddenly, I began to realize how profound wise old Zizi's take on life was and the value of her lifetime of knowledge. The things we talked about and the strength of her convictions compelled me to think about who we are as everyday people and to question the quality of our lives as we move into the twenty-first century.

It was May 1999, the perfect time to begin this true story.

Don't Save All Your Money for a Rainy Day

H ello, beautiful," I said in my best Latin-lover voice. "I simply *must* see you tonight."

"How I would love that, Honeyboy," Zizi replied mischievously. "But I've got a hot date."

"Well, tell him that you have a headache," I said. "I'm downtown and I'll be there around five."

Zizi's house in Yonkers is about a half-hour drive from midtown Manhattan. It was 3:30, so I'd have enough time to go to the Italian deli on Arthur Avenue in the Bronx and pick up some homemade sausage, mozzarella, ricotta cheese, and a napoleon. Zizi loves napoleons with their rich cream and layers of thin pastry topped off with swirls of vanilla and chocolate icing. I crossed the street to the garage that held my car, took off my jacket, put down the top, and with Count Basie providing the entertainment, I was off to visit my eighty-three-year-old aunt, who is widowed and lives alone.

People say to me, "How nice it is that you visit your aunt." I say to them, "How nice it is that I have an aunt like Zizi to visit." Although I've been close to her all my life, our bond grew stronger following the death of her husband in 1992 and the death of my marriage in 1996. In the dark days, months, and years following my divorce, while I suffered from depression and a broken heart, Zizi became my lifesaver, a calm port in my emotional storm. No matter what hour of the day I turned up at her house she would always be there, welcoming me with open arms, ready to talk or listen. Much of the time, though, we did little of either. We would eat Zizi's sumptuous Italian meals and play Scrabble.

"Scrabble is good for you," Zizi said when she first pulled out the game. "To play you have to concentrate on making words, so you won't have time to concentrate on your sorrows." In the beginning, though, I would often manage to concentrate on both. That gradually changed, but the results of the game invariably did not. If I didn't concentrate on the game she would beat me, and if I did concentrate on the game she would beat me.

"After you're dead and gone, I'm going to tell everyone that I let you win," I'd often tease Zizi.

"If you do I'll haunt you from heaven," she'd reply with a warning wave of her finger.

Now, five years and several hundred Scrabble games later, I can honestly say that if it weren't for all the love, caring, and wisdom that I got from Zizi, I don't know how I would have healed.

Zizi's house is a modest redbrick and gray fieldstone ranch on a tree-lined street in one of the nicer sections of Yonkers. On this beautiful day, I knew I'd find her sitting in a canvas director's chair on the back porch soaking up the sun and puffing away on a cigarette. When she saw me walk up the flagstone path, Zizi quickly snuffed out the butt and held her arms outstretched. "Oh, Gerald, I'm so happy to see you! It's so wonderful that you come to visit your aunt," she said as she showered me with a flurry of loud kisses on both cheeks. "You're a good boy, you bring such joy to my life. I know how busy you are and I'm so thankful that you spend so much time with me."

"Are you kidding, Zizi?" I said, bending down to give her a hug. "I don't know what I would do without you."

While I went into the house to put away the food that I bought and change into more casual clothes, Zizi stayed on the porch to smoke another cigarette. About five feet tall and shrinking ("Are you getting taller or am I getting shorter?" she sometimes asks me), Zizi fits into the typical Italian-mama classification—plump and cuddly. Her hair, once thick and jet-black, has aged into a sparse crop of silver ringlets, and her soft eyes reflect a lifetime of emotions but droop a bit more toward sadness than joy. A slight point at the tip of her triangular chin defines a face that seems better proportioned for the petite figure she had as a young woman.

By the time I returned, Zizi had moved inside to the kitchen, a cozy room decked out with her grandchildren's artwork and an assortment of holy objects—a braided sheaf of palm, a cherished image of the Sacred Heart, and a needlepoint of the Twenty-third Psalm, the one that begins "The Lord is my shepherd, I shall not want. . . ." As soon as I walked into the kitchen, I felt Zizi's deep warmth and breathed in the bouquet of magic seasonings that have helped nourish the souls and feed the hearts of her family, relatives, and friends for nearly fifty years. This kitchen has a history . . . it's been lived in!

"What were you doing in the city?" Zizi asked. She was seated in her usual place, in a captain's-style chair at the small Formica kitchen table, her body twisted toward a little black-and-white TV that had been blaring in the background since I arrived.

Noticing the sink full of pots, pans, and dishes, I picked up the sponge and detergent and began to wash them as I started to answer her question. But before I could turn on the water, she interrupted. "Stop!" she said. "You're my guest. Don't wash the dishes. Sit down and talk to me."

"Okay," I said, but I continued to scrub away and began to tell her what I was doing in Manhattan. CNN was running a series on the third millennium. I've been a trend forecaster for over twenty years and head up The Trends Research Institute in Rhinebeck, New York, which is about two hours north of New York City. As publisher of the *Trends Journal* and author of the book *Trends 2000*, I was asked by CNN and other media for my take on the meaning of the new millennium and my forecasts of what the future would hold. One reason they call on me is that I've developed a respectable track record of picking business, consumer, political, and economic trends before they come to pass. The future doesn't happen in a vacuum. Just as the decisions we make in our personal lives determine our destiny, the same holds true for society. There are implications for everything we do. Each action has a reaction. It's my job to see how the issues and events of today will determine the trends of tomorrow.

I started to tell Zizi that I was concerned about what I could see coming up on the horizon, and began to explain why so much of our everyday life would change—for better and for worse. But it was fast becoming a one-sided conversation. While Zizi's eyesight is still 20/20, her hearing is gradually getting worse. And with the TV blaring and the water running as I washed the dishes, it was a challenge for her to hear me.

"Forget what's going to happen in the future. Sit down. I want to look at you," Zizi commanded. Raising her voice a notch, she again ordered me to stop washing the dishes. "I'll do them when you leave. I want to talk to you. I don't want to waste the time we're together watching you stand at the sink."

Since my divorce, I hadn't been cooking much for myself, so when I came to visit she would not only cook a huge diet-busting meal for me to eat there, but also prepare enough food for another week for me to take home. I could tell by the stacks of pots and pans that she had been busy trying to get every-thing ready before I arrived. "You can look at me from where you're sitting," I joked. "I'm almost finished."

"Don't get smart! Come over here now!" she said in a stern but playful voice.

"Okay, Zizi, you win," I said with a smile. I had cleaned the dishes and put most of them away. I dried my hands with the crumpled dish towel that lay on the counter, and pulled up a chair across from her.

Zizi can hardly walk. She relies more and more on her alu-minum walker to help her shuffle around the house. All my life I remember her constantly suffering from severe phlebitis, a chronic inflammation of the veins that affects both her legs. There is no delicate way to describe what her legs look like. They are covered with oozing sores; the layers of skin have evaporated to a translucent membrane that appears stretched to the limit as bulging veins and arteries struggle to break through. It's been years since she's been able to wear regular shoes. Beneath the loose floor-length dresses she wears, her terribly swollen feet are stuffed into an extra-wide pair of sneakers. Being on her feet is painful, so whenever I visit I try to do what I can, like clean up her kitchen. For all her pain and discomfort, only rarely does she ever complain. And she tries to avoid the doctor. A series of butchered leg operations performed years ago has left her hospital-phobic and doctor-wary.

Recently, with her condition rapidly deteriorating, I had to push her to seek treatment. For several weeks the open sores had been worsening. "Honeyboy, it feels like there are worms of steel moving through my legs," she said softly. The visit to the doctor helped. He put her on a course of antibiotics and other medications. The pain eased and the symptoms stopped. "Thank God the sores are healing a bit," she said with a sense of cautious relief. "The doctor told me that if they didn't get better I'd have to go into the hospital."

Zizi is from the old school. Like most people of her generation she had put her trust in the "good doctor's" hands and looked up to him as a demigod. But that belief began to change more than a half century ago when Zizi had her first child. It was 1940, and the autumn leaves had just begun to fall, when Alfred Charles Villane was born. That's the name that appears on the birth certificate, and that's when the trouble began. In what turned out to be not such a good move, Zizi named the baby after her husband, Alfred. The problem was that in the custom of traditional Italian families, it is ordained that the first boy is to be named after the father's father. But Zizi didn't like her father-in-law's name, Cosmo. When Zizi's mother-in-law found out the baby had been named Alfred, she marched over to the hospital in a rage and read Zizi the riot act. Instead of celebrating the birth of the family's firstborn, Grandma Villane brought misery to the young couple. Zizi was branded a "traitor" by her mother-in-law and coincidentally—or not—it was then that this young woman with the legs of a model and the soul of a swing dancer began to develop phlebitis.

To help put out the fire and end the feud, Zizi's mother, a woman of peace, suggested that Zizi baptize her baby Cosmo Christopher: Cosmo after the father-in-law and Christopher after Columbus—since he was born on Columbus Day. Grandma told her that, unlike the formalities of Italy, in America people are often called by nicknames. She reasoned that before long, they'd be calling the little boy Chris. Zizi agreed and certainly understood what her mother meant. Born in 1915 in Altavilla Irpina, Italy, her own name, Filomena, which means "full of laughter," had become Americanized to Phyllis. They baptized the baby as Cosmo.

In the greater scheme of things, the name of Zizi's baby meant nothing. What mattered was that Cosmo would die before his second birthday, and Zizi would never know why.

Cosmo had a high fever and his stomach felt rigid. Fearing it was peritonitis—a potentially deadly infection that could have been caused by a ruptured appendix—the doctor immediately operated. After the operation the doctor said it wasn't peritonitis after all, but serious complications resulted from the operation. He told Zizi that he had made a mistake. Cosmo was in critical condition for several weeks.

Each time Zizi tells the story of the botched operation and how she watched her Cosmo slowly die—from a distance—I can see from the pain on her face the truth in the statement that there is nothing more painful for a parent than to lose a child.

"What did I know at twenty-three years old? I was only a kid," she told me, more sad than angry. "The nurses wouldn't let me hold my baby."

Under strict orders, for the two months that Cosmo was in the hospital, neither Zizi, Uncle Al, nor any other member of the family was allowed to go into the children's ward where he lay in his crib. "Every day I'd go to the hospital, but all I could do was look at him from behind a glass partition," she told me, lamenting how "stupid" she was for obeying orders and not demanding to be next to her baby. "I knew better. I knew my baby needed me as much as I needed him. My instincts told me the doctor was wrong but I was afraid to fight back."

"Zizi, it was the times," I'd reassure her. "You did the best you could."

When we look back at the "good old days," we often do it wearing rose-colored glasses. We tend to forget the inequities and discrimination that also made them the "bad old days." Nostalgia distorts our view of history. Some things are better left in the past, such as the way a doctor's word was revered as gospel.

The attitude of arrogance and air of infallibility that surrounded the medical profession back then had also taken its toll on my family. Around 1950, my twelve-year-old sister Grace, the second oldest of seven children, fell off her bike and broke her arm. The doctor put the limb in a full cast and, to help get the bones back in place, then put her arm in traction. But in his haste, he placed the traction bar on top of her thumb instead of under it. Grace complained continually, but the doctor and nurses ignored her cries. My parents bowed to the doctor who ridiculed my sister for crying so much. After a week or so, my father knew something was wrong. He went to the hospital and despite protests from the doctor, he disconnected Grace's arm from traction. But it was too late. When my father cut off the cast, her thumb fell off. The pressure from the traction bar had cut off circulation, causing gangrene to set in. Poor Grace had lost about a third of her hand.

When I think of little Cosmo I can't help but wonder how hopeless, stranded, and isolated this innocent child must have felt. Would it have made a difference in his recovery if he had been cradled close to his mother's breast and showered with her affection? Would little Cosmo's will to survive have been heightened by his loving father's singing voice, the caresses and care that would pour from the hearts of his grandmas and grandpas and all his aunts and uncles who loved him so much?

Zizi said that had she been wiser and older she'd have told

both the doctor and nurse to go to hell. "If only they had penicillin back then. I wonder if Cosmo would be alive today," Zizi said. "He was such a beautiful baby, with a complexion like fine china, curly blond hair, and royal blue eyes. People would stop me to tell me how beautiful *she* was. 'He's a little *boy*,' I would tell them."

Baby Cosmo

Whenever Zizi tells the story of Cosmo, she always says he was too perfect for this world. She's not exaggerating. Right there in the hallway, as soon as you come into her house, is a picture of Baby Cosmo hanging next to those of her other four children. Every time I look at his photo I say to myself, "His complexion looks like fine china."

"The night before Cosmo passed on," Zizi said, "I had a dream that he had died. Early next morning the hospital called to tell me to come over right away. It was a dark and dreary day—like a hurricane was about to strike, when Alfred, Grandma, Uncle Nicky, and I got to the hospital. Cosmo was lying motionless in the crib, when he slowly opened his beautiful eyes and pointed to a chain with a medal of the Blessed Mother that was hanging from the railing of the bed. As Grandma put the medal in his outstretched hand, he reached over with his other hand for a small picture of Saint Anthony that hung next to him. At the very moment Cosmo grasped the picture and the medal, his eyes closed and suddenly the sun burst out. It was so bright it was almost blinding. Then, in the next instant, the weather turned pitch dark again. I believe that at the moment of the sunburst, the heavens opened up to accept Cosmo. God wanted an angel and he took him."

Cosmo's death took more than just an emotional toll on Zizi and Uncle Al. It ruined them financially.

"Gerald, you know how they tell you to save money for a

rainy day? I used to believe that," Zizi told me. "Well, when your uncle and I got married in 1939 we had saved five thousand dollars. That was a lot of money back then. But in the two months that Cosmo was in the hospital, it all went to the doctors. Don't save all your money for a rainy day because you may end up spending it all on rain. Spend some on sunshine. Enjoy life."

And boy did it rain. My uncle Al had opened a butcher shop in the Bronx just before Cosmo was born and business was pretty good. While little Cosmo was being laid to rest, Uncle Al's shop was robbed. They cleaned him out—from cash register to wrapping paper; they stole everything that wasn't nailed down. And, just as Zizi and Uncle Al had no health insurance, they weren't insured against burglary.

Without asking Zizi, Uncle Al sold what was left of his business for only $700. When he came home and told Zizi what he had done, she couldn't believe it. "Al, why did you do such a thing?" she asked him, hoping that somehow it wasn't true. "I had to pay the undertaker," he sullenly replied. "That's how much we owed him."

It was 1942. World War II was raging. My father was a foreman in the shipyards and was able to get Uncle Al a job working nights in a maintenance crew. During the day Zizi had a job sewing buttons on army jackets. When one of them was coming home, the other one was going to work. But even when they were able to spend time together, the silence of sadness separated them. The tension began to ease several months after Cosmo passed on, when Zizi became pregnant again.

Not a day goes by that Zizi doesn't say a prayer for Cosmo and feel the deep sorrow of his loss. She also prays for the souls of all the loved ones who have departed, believing that those who have passed on welcome our prayers . . . and often need them. It's a practice I've taken up as well. I find that when I pray for my wonderful parents, aunts, uncles, and friends who are gone, it reminds me of the love we shared, how fortunate I was to have lived life with them, and how thankful I am for all the richness they gave.

"Count your blessings one by one," Zizi tells me, "and you'll see all that God has done."

"Come here," she said, holding her arms open. "I want to give you a kiss."

God Can Lift the Hurt You're Feeling

I love the way Zizi hugs and squeezes me. Not only because I can feel her affection, but also because the "squeeze test" is my private diagnostic technique. I never told Zizi, but I gauge how healthy she feels by how tight she hugs me. I learned over the years that when she's feeling run-down, the squeezes weaken.

"You're so good to your old aunt," she said. I kissed her on both cheeks and looked at her while tears filled her eyes—and mine—as I thought about all of the goodness she has brought into my life.

"Your beautiful smile is back, Honeyboy, and so is your spirit," Zizi said as I returned to my chair. She was referring to the sadness that had overwhelmed me since my divorce.

In business terms, they'd call our relationship a win-win situation. Zizi and I are members of a mutual admiration society. "I'm doing fine, Zizi, you know how it is," I said. "Some days are better than others but most of them are really good."

"That's about the best you can expect out of life," Zizi assured me. She paused. "Even so, Jerry, I wish Alfred were still alive."

Her husband, my uncle Al, whom we called "the Dude," died several years ago of a heart attack, leaving Zizi with plenty of debt and no savings.

Zizi says that even though she and Uncle Al had their tough times together they always worked things out. "It takes devotion to keep a marriage together—it's never smooth or easy for anyone. I believe that by working through the trying times and learning from the struggles it helps make you stronger and wiser," Zizi told me. "But most people today are different—when the water gets too rough they're ready to bail out."

I knew this all too well. My own marriage of twenty-three years was scuttled on a warm, sunny Valentine's Day, when my wife told me she no longer loved me, was no longer interested in working things out, and wasn't going to stick around until death do us part. So, despite my pleas and pledges to do anything possible to salvage all that we had built together, two days later she packed her bags and walked out. Her sudden departure hit me like a death blow. We used to say we were like two peas in a pod. We worked together, cooked together, gardened. . . . We spent most of our lives doing nearly everything together. When she walked out I knew my life could never be the same. She was the only woman I had ever loved. I was so committed in my heart that I could not imagine living without her.

Over time, left only with my memories, I began to see the many mistakes I had made in my marriage. "Making mistakes is a way of learning," Zizi reminded me when I would beat up on myself. "No one in this world is perfect. Admit what you've done and don't repeat it."

For me, it wasn't that easy. More than just being heartsick from the loss of my partner in life, I felt a deep pain acknowledging how my actions and behavior over the years helped push my wife away. No matter what I'd do or where I was, I couldn't escape the sadness and remorse that tortured me. At night, instead of sleeping, I would fill my mind with haunting memories that I played over and over like a broken record.

Childless, and with both parents deceased, I was fortunate to have a few good friends to turn to and Zizi to comfort me. Yet despite their caring I would become so distraught that I felt suicidal at times, even to the extent of planning for the most painless way out. When I told Zizi of my desperate thoughts, she said I would be "playing into the hands of the devil" if I carried out my dark urges. "Satan wants you to kill yourself because he wants your soul," she said as the sparkle in her eyes dimmed. "And if you killed yourself, it would kill me too."

To comfort me Zizi gave me this poem she wrote for a broken heart.

HEARTBREAK AND HEALING

God can lift the hurt you're feeling
He can take away each care
but, you must give him your burdens
and that's only done through prayer.
God knows everything about you
from beginning to end.
He can help you like no other,
He's your very dearest friend.
Ill hearts can break, they're fragile as glass
but God will mend them, and this too shall pass.
Follow your rainbows, follow your dream.
And don't let your sorrows keep you downstream.
After the storm, bright rainbows appear.
Leave your teardrops behind, there's nothing to fear.
Our crosses are blessings that come in disguise
God's love and God's purpose, let's try to recognize.

"I was married for fifty-two years," Zizi offered, "and believe me, there were many times I would have liked to leave the old goat, but we stuck it out. Your uncle was eccentric and had his ways, but he was a loving husband, a good father, and a hardworking man. I remember after we'd have a terrible argument, he would apologize and say, 'Phyllis, I'll do anything for you, I would even swim an ocean for you.' I knew he was full of it because he didn't know how to swim."

It was 1938 when Zizi met Uncle Al. A year earlier my grandfather had moved his family from 117th Street in Italian Harlem to the Bronx. One night Grandma asked Zizi to go with her to meet some paesanos from her village in Italy who had just moved into the neighborhood. Grandma had her roots in Florence, but Grandpa was born and raised in Altavilla Irpina, a little hilltop village about sixty miles southeast of Naples.

"I remember that night like it was yesterday," Zizi said, recalling how she and Uncle Al met. "I thought he was a grump and I really didn't like him at first. We were all talking in the kitchen that evening and he was in the other room listening to opera. He asked us to lower our voices because it was interfering with the music.

"His sister Mary had gone to a wedding the day before and couldn't stop talking about how great the band was and what a wonderful time she had dancing. Mary asked me if I liked to dance and would I like to dance with her. I loved to dance and in those days it was common for women to dance together, even at home. So she asked Al to turn off the opera and put on a swing record. After a few dances Mary said to Al, 'Dance with her, she's really good.'

"He took me in his arms, we went around a few times, and before the music was over he said to me, 'Lady, you're dynamite.' The next year we were married. How different the times were back then. I believed it was a sin to have sex before I got married and Al was afraid to try anything because my father would have killed him.

Zizi and Al

"Oh, how I miss him, Jerry," she said, dabbing her eyes with a crumbled tissue.

ALFRED

I'm exceptionally blue today.
I can't seem to make my tears
go away.
Thinking of Alfred all day long
Please good Lord make me strong
We took our lives for granted
Thinking we would never part
But all I have are memories and
a broken heart.
I know your spirit is around me
because I feel it so
How I miss you, you'll never know.

Golden Years
Can Bring Tears

I miss Uncle Al, too. When I was a kid he would take my cousin Ronnie, his son, and my two brothers, Tony and Bobby, and me to Yankee Stadium. Those were the days when Mickey Mantle, Phil Rizzuto, Yogi Berra, Whitey Ford, and other Yankee greats packed the lineup. I remember the thrill as we'd run up the ramps to our grandstand seats on those sunny Sunday afternoons. The grand ol' "House That Ruth Built" had a magical air of excitement that was lost in the 1970s makeover of the stadium.

Ronnie and I, being only a year apart, were more like brothers. As soon as we were ushered to our seats he and I would take off and scour the stands for any piece of paper we could find. Then, we'd feverishly shred it up, ready to toss the confetti into the air to celebrate the next big play. It seemed that the stands were always packed and the Yankees never lost.

Uncle Al would buy us the obligatory hot dog, soda, and peanuts, and my folks would give us boys a dollar each to spend as we wished. I still have some old souvenir photos of those great Yankee ballplayers.

When we'd get home Uncle Al would say to my brothers and me, "Who's your favorite uncle?" and Zizi would say, "Al, don't ask them that, they love *all* their uncles." She was right. We loved them all and no matter how much he'd tease us we'd never say "Uncle Al."

In later years, he and I would take long weekend trips to visit Ron, who lived several hours away in upstate New York. From the moment Uncle Al got in my car we'd listen to 1930s and '40s jazz tapes, joke around, and wouldn't stop laughing until the weekend was over. "Why, you turkey, you," he'd say to me in his patented W. C. Fields–type voice, when I'd do something goofy. Alfred Villane was one of a kind and everyone who had known him would readily agree that after he was born they threw away the mold.

"He was colorful," Zizi said.

Uncle Al eventually opened up another butcher shop after the war and had a good business until the 1960s. But he died broke and it was really heartbreaking.

"You know, Gerald, your uncle was overcautious," Zizi told me. "And he wasn't very flexible. I kept urging him to expand the business and go in new directions. I told him that times were changing and soon people would be going to supermarkets to buy their meats and do all their shopping. I could see the handwriting on the wall as more and more women started to go to work. I knew that people wouldn't have time to shop and prepare meals like they did in my day. But he wouldn't listen. He was from the old school and believed that people would always demand quality meats and cook big meals.

"Thank God I have this house, it's the only thing I own," she said. "I could get myself sick if I dwelled on being alone and on my other problems. I'm thankful for all that I have been blessed with. Good memories are treasures."

Not one to dwell on the negative, Zizi has a remarkable capacity to instantly shift her mental gears when being dragged down by a depressing thought. Having seen her do it time and time again, I'm convinced that this attitude is more than a mental elixir. It keeps her alive.

Zizi's financial circumstances could mirror those of your aunt, uncle, mother, father, or any old person who is living alone and on a shoestring. She clips coupons to save thirty-five cents on a pound of butter or twenty-five cents on two rolls of toilet paper. She lives off the several hundred dollars a month she gets from Social Security, and is routinely forced to decide whether to buy drugs or buy food. Zizi is part of a generation that is mostly ignored except when they can be exploited by

TV, in advertisements, or by the news media. You know the familiar scenes: those happily bungling or quick-witted old folks featured on the soaps and sitcoms; the cure-all drug ads for arthritis and the Viagra-induced bliss promoted by Bob Dole; or the lost-in-space antics of Senator John Glenn.

I remember how disgusted Zizi was by the heavy media coverage of seventy-seven-year-old Glenn's return to space. They featured it as though it were one of the most important events of our lifetime. "That wasn't a space trip, it was an ego trip," Zizi said. "What's he looking for up there? And what did he bring back? The money would be better spent giving it to the poor. And now he wants to go up in space again. *A fa Napoli!*" she cried. (The term implies that a person is full of baloney. Rather than tell them to go to hell, you tell them to go to Naples.)

If you look at the elderly through the eyes of the media you would think that the "golden years" are being enjoyed by happy-go-lucky retirees who have nothing to do in life but decide where to eat their "early-bird special," which cruise to take, or whether to sign up for an "Over 70 and Feeling Fit Cross-Country Bike Tour."

That's not what America really looks like. We are a first-, second-, and third-world nation all wrapped up into one. Sure there are the hearty, the healthy, and the financially secure, but they are a minority of our population. Our country is filled with tens of millions of old people living on their own: the helpless in nursing homes, the shut-ins wallowing in the depths of poverty, or the one million in hospice care just waiting—or wanting—to die.

Getting old is tough enough, but getting old in America is getting tougher. It's estimated that the average sixty-five-year-old has a 43 percent chance of ending up in a nursing home. But "nursing home" is another one of those phrases that doesn't really mean what it says. Essentially just holding pens, most are devoid of nursing. Our government says nursing homes should have enough registered nurses to provide each inmate at least twelve minutes a day of "care," but only 31 percent of the homes even meet that substandard measure.

If an elderly person had it bad before going into a nursing home, the odds are good that the situation will get a lot worse once committed ("committed" is a polite word; "sentenced" is more appropriate). Even as complaints of abuse rise, state and federal authorities routinely ignore them. One-fourth of the nation's 17,000 nursing homes are in such bad shape that simply living in a facility caused "immediate jeopardy or actual harm" to residents, the General Accounting Office reported.

Zizi's children are concerned about her living alone and want her to move in with them. But she's adamant about being on her own. She loves her little house and is convinced she'll be there until her dying days. She's also fortunate to have three of her children living close by. They help out and do what they can, but with their own children to raise, heavy work schedules, household expenses, and problems of their own, it's barely enough, so I try to fill in the financial gaps.

As for those families who have their elderly loved ones living at home, forget it. What has been called a "sandwich" generation, some 25 million caregivers—mostly women—who are still raising their own children, is now being sandwiched financially, emotionally, and physically with the added pressure of providing care to elderly and often ill parents. And we haven't seen the worst of it. Wait until the baby boomers hit the old-age circuit. Often single, divorced, childless, or with small or no families, many aging boomers will be on their own and out of luck. When they hit retirement age most will be without pensions or adequate retirement plans. And that's the least of it. The nation is ignoring looming trends that will put even heavier pressures on our already weakened health care system when the 78 million boomers succumb to old age and a host of chronic degenerative diseases.

Zizi is the last of a breed that was around when it was still common to live in an extended family household—three generations living under one roof. Before moving to Yonkers in the mid-1950s, she lived with Uncle Al and the kids on the second floor of my grandparents' house on Matthews Avenue in the Bronx.

"I don't want to live with my kids," Zizi tells me, though she used to live with her parents when she and Al were starting out. "When we lived in Grandpa and Grandma's house, life was different. It's hard to imagine when you see what the Bronx looks like today, but I can remember the little farm behind their house. Grandpa had a wonderful vegetable garden, raised rabbits, cured sausages, and made wine, just like he did back in the old country.

"It seemed as though Grandma and Grandpa were always cooking," Zizi continued. "Friends and family were always stopping by and there was always food on the table. Every night your dad would come visit Grandma and have a cup of espresso with her.

"Uncle Harry had hooked up a buzzer between Grandma's bedroom and mine. Every morning, around six forty-five, she would buzz to let me know that she was awake and that it was time for me to get the children ready for school. I can still picture her giving Ronnie a kiss as he left for school, saying, '*La Madonna ti compagna,*' May the Blessed Mother accompany you.

"One morning it was around five to seven and I noticed that she didn't buzz. About ten after seven it started buzzing and buzzing. I went downstairs to her bedroom and I'll never forget the picture. Grandpa was standing over Grandma holding a cup of espresso with tears streaming down his cheeks. She had died. He used to bring her coffee in bed every morning for forty-five years.

"The only reason Al and I moved was that it was too hard for me to stay there with all those memories. Besides, Uncle

Uncles Frankie, Nicky, and Harry, entertaining Grandma

Nicky had just gotten married, and I knew he and Aunt Helen, who was pregnant, needed the apartment more than we did."

Zizi and my cousins tell me that the years spent living with my grandparents were the happiest of their lives.

By the 1950s the American family began to shift into the modern "nuclear" form. Mom and Dad no longer lived where they had grown up. Today, the "splintered" family is becoming more common, and with so many single and divorced parents and broken families scattered across the country, most of the elderly will be on their own or at the mercy of the government for help.

I'm often reminded of when I was a teenager, my dad saying to me more than once, "Son, in this country, one father can take care of seven children, but seven children can't take care of one father."

Sometimes I'm asked where I learned to track trends, since it's not a profession taught in school. My father gave me my basic training. A visionary, he passed on to me the skills he used to analyze the events of the present to see how and why they would shape the future. Each Saturday, in order to give my mother a break, since I was known as a "terror," he'd take me with him to work. In those days he had a construction company, so I got to go with him "on business." During our conversations he would tease me anytime I would repeat the standard line about an issue or event that was popular or making the news. "*Pappagallo*, parrot, don't repeat what everyone else is saying. Think for yourself," he'd say. The message sank in.

My dad's observations about the elderly in America were on the mark. Emerson made an observation similar to my father's when he wrote, "You can tell the morals of a society by how it treats its old." In America there is little appreciation, respect, and dignity afforded to our elderly. Rather than being revered for their wisdom and appreciated for their contributions, they are treated as burdens to society.

Every year, around budget time, politicians rail against "entitlements" that help feed, house, clothe, and educate people. Any government program that can improve the quality of living is attacked as a budget-busting villain. The president and Congress talk as if everyday people aren't "entitled" to an equitable payback after putting in a lifetime of work and paying a lifetime of taxes. And like clockwork, under the guise of balancing the budget, politicians cut funding or hold the line on the quality of life programs that ease burdens or provide some pleasure for the "little people"—as billionaire Leona Helmsley referred to us average Americans—who are forced to pay taxes.

"Forget what anyone has ever told you before about the 'golden years,' " Zizi said. "Getting old is no fun . . . what's this 'gold' they talk about? It's more like a mixture of tin and lead. Old people are like old cars. You fix one thing and something else breaks. At the end you have to junk it."

Zizi recited this little poem to express her feelings.

GOLDEN YEARS CAN BRING TEARS

I look in the mirror and
what do I see
A sad old lady staring at me.
With skin so wrinkled
and my hair so gray
I can't believe I've become this way.

Running her fingers through her sparse crop of hair, Zizi reflected on her youth. "You know, Honeyboy, I wasn't always an old duck. You wouldn't know it now but I once had a great shape: 36-24-36. When I was about seventeen years old, your mother and I went up to 125th Street to the RKO Proctors to see a movie and a stage show.

"Your mother and I were best friends. The only time I got angry with your mom," Zizi said, "was just before she got married and we were both working. I told her not to wear a new dress I bought. Well, she wore it anyway and got ink on the sleeve. I got so upset that I told her to keep it because I would never wear it again.

"Anyway, as we were walking into RKO, a man stopped and asked me to step aside. He said they were running a contest and asked if they could take a picture of me. 'Only a picture?' I asked. 'Yes,' he promised, 'nothing else.' "

A few weeks later Zizi received a letter saying that she had been chosen to compete in a national beauty pageant. She would have to pack a bathing suit and clothing for two weeks for the big contest in Atlantic City. "All excited, I told my father what had happened and showed him the letter. Did he hit the ceiling! 'What are you—crazy?' He said to me, 'You want to go away for two weeks and parade your legs in front of everybody? What are you—out of your mind? You can't go. *Camina!* Go take a walk!' That was that. I didn't go. Things were different in those days. Maybe it wasn't something for a

Zizi at age seventeen

seventeen-year-old girl to do. Who knows? Maybe my life would have turned out very differently had I gone."

While Zizi's face at eighty-three expresses a lifetime of gentleness, love, and kindness, it's hard for me to find the features of that seventeen-year-old etched in her face today. What will always shine through, though, is her spirit and her heart. These things have never—and will never—change.

How About Voting
for the Better
of Two Goods?

Politicians keep milking the *great to be alive in the land of riches* myth, and every election they jockey for poll position by promising to fight for working Americans. With the political campaigns starting to heat up, I wanted to know which candidate Zizi believed held out the best hope of delivering on their promises.

"Who are you going to vote for?" I asked Zizi. "Who's your favorite?"

The slack-jawed stare Zizi gave me was the look you get from someone when you ask a dumb question that has an obvious answer.

"I won't vote for any of them," Zizi replied. "I agree with your dear mother, may her soul rest in peace," she continued.

"One time we were shopping in the Bronx and there was a politician handing out pamphlets to a small crowd. Your mother walked up to the man and said, 'You're all a bunch of liars . . . you'll say anything to get elected.' "

I laughed, because my mom had done the same thing with me. In Getty Square in Yonkers, when I was about twelve years old, she walked up to a man campaigning for office and said, "You're a phony just like the rest of them." Was I embarrassed!

Each Election Day, Zizi's cynicism about politics gets a boost when someone from the Democratic party calls and offers to pick her up at home and drive her to the polling place. "Every year," Zizi said, "I tell the person, 'Don't bother me. I'm disgusted with the whole bunch of you. If you want to drive me somewhere, drive me to the supermarket so I can do some shopping.' "

"Listen, Zizi," I replied, "if you don't vote, then you can't complain about who got elected. You get what you deserve."

Zizi laughed. "Listen, Gerald, I've been hearing that line for years. At one time there was a difference between the two parties and I'd always vote. Grandpa was so proud to be an American that he'd be first on line at the polling place. Voters had a real choice. The Democrats were the party of the working people and the Republicans favored businesspeople. Today there's only about a dime's worth of difference between them, and a dime today isn't worth a penny."

I told Zizi that I saw her point. "When I was a kid, my

father told me that the Democrats will get you into war and the Republicans will put you in a depression. Now either party is capable of doing both!"

"And speaking of money, who do they think they're fooling?" Zizi continued. "The only people politicians represent are the ones who give them the most money. You've got to be rich or backed by the rich to run for office in America today—it's a monopoly."

"It's a plutocracy, Zizi. That's what you call a nation that is run by the wealthy," I replied. Facts are facts. The price tag for Campaign 2000 was over $3 billion. At just one fund-raiser George W. Bush took in $20 million, while Gore helped bag $26 million for "the party." At a very extortionate price, the entrenched powers have closed the doors on democracy. When challengers try to unseat incumbents, the incumbents win 98 percent of the time!

"Call it what you want, Jerry, but today's political system is so corrupt that I won't vote anymore." Zizi is among the 50 percent of eligible voters who don't vote.

"Zizi!" was all I could reply. But there was no swaying her.

"Would you worship a religion you didn't believe in?" Zizi asked me.

"No," I quickly answered.

"Would you go to their church and recite their prayers and give money to a religion that you didn't believe in?"

"No."

"Then why would you expect me to kneel at the altar of a political religion I don't believe in?" Zizi asked. With that, she put the crochet hooks and yarn on the table into a worn shopping bag that held a half-finished blanket.

Crocheting helps Zizi avoid smoking. Plus, it keeps her mind busy. "When my legs got so bad that I couldn't walk, I knew I'd have to do something to keep from getting depressed. So I taught myself to crochet. My mother was a sewing teacher and a fine seamstress. When we were children she gave your mother and me crochet needles and taught us how to make a chain—in and out, in and out. The better I got, the more fun I had. The more fun I had, the more things I made."

Zizi gives away everything she makes. Sometimes when I go visit her and mention one of my friends in conversation, she'll ask, "Does he cook?" If the answer is yes, she instantly gives me two pot holders to pass along. I have a houseload of her handicrafts, including an earth-tone bedcover embroidered with yellow and red flowers. It's great having things that Zizi's made, because they remind me of her.

One winter, Alex, the young cousin of a woman I had been dating, came from France to visit. It was wet and blustery when she arrived in New York, and the poor little girl came down with a terrible cold. My girlfriend had received a hat and scarf set as a gift from Zizi and gave it to Alex to keep her warm. Alex loved the light lavender ensemble, wore it everywhere, and took it back to France where she was attending fashion school. Recently, during my visit to Paris, Alex told me that every time she wears Zizi's hat and scarf, all her friends want to know how they can get them. Alex tells them that she got them in New York from "Fashions by Zizi," and that Zizi has a very exclusive clientele.

"Listen, Gerald," Zizi said, getting back to the politics. "Why should I vote for a 'lesser of two evils'? It's one of the dumbest ideas I ever heard in my life. Imagine admitting that you actually take time out of your life to vote for a 'lesser of two evils.' How about voting for the better of two goods?"

I'd never thought of it quite like that. Each election we hear the same story repeated by the majority of voters who say: "I voted for so-and-so because he's the lesser of two evils." I've never heard anyone say, "Boy, I had a tough choice in the voting booth yesterday . . . I couldn't decide who to vote for. Both candidates were really terrific." Isn't that a radical concept?

Still, I see things differently from Zizi. Perhaps more optimistically. I believe that within the decade, there will be a real third-party movement in America that will challenge what has essentially become a two-headed one-party system. I call this movement the "progressive-libertarian party." It will serve as a counterbalance to those favoring free-for-all globalization. It will combine progressive economic and social philosophies with libertarian approaches to privacy and foreign policy involvement. Its platform will be built around immigration, trade, sovereignty, and environmental issues. It will also address public fears about affordable, quality health care, food safety, and retirement security.

What makes me believe this will happen? The progressive-libertarian banner will be carried by members of the Millennium Generation who, at seventy-three million strong, are rich in high-tech knowledge, are financially capable, and possess the youthful stamina and zeal needed to effect change. Born between 1978 and 1995, this is the first generation to be indoctrinated from birth with pro-environment attitudes. They have anticorporate sentiments from witnessing the broken bonds between employers and employees. They've been bombarded by a stream of events—from Monica Lewinsky and impeachment to campaign finance corruption—that have left them feeling betrayed and without respect for political office and officeholders. They are also the first socially active generation since the boomers in the 1960s. They protest against sweatshops, unrestricted free trade, animal rights abuses; and, they voice support for a variety of prolabor issues and environmental causes.

This may sound like the rhetoric of the Woodstock Generation, but there's a difference. Unlike in the sixties, when antiwar and social protests galvanized the baby boomers against their parents, today the Millennium Generation and their baby-boomer parents are reading from the same page when it comes to most social and political issues. Back in the sixties a psychological gulf separated the generations. Today there is little dis-agreement between children and parents on the issues of the day. It's a trend I call "Generation Blending."

In my lifetime, and probably over the lifetime of this nation, there has never before been such a blending of issues and ideals between two generational powerhouses. Joining together, these 140 million–plus like-minded agents for change will be unstoppable in their mission to bring "power to the people." In the near future a galvanizing issue—war, racism, economic destabilization—will spark this revolution-in-waiting and unite these generations into action.

This blending of generations and their unified effort toward achieving a common societal benefit could also serve to offset the shortcomings that are part of each. We've been inundated with the idea that the greatest generation was that which fought valiantly in World War II and worked tirelessly to build a strong America. It is a credit to them for all they endured, the sacrifices they made, the hardships with which they were burdened and their inner strength, which proved that they had what it took to succeed where other countries failed. But the history of the world is much too complex for a single generation to have been the greatest or to be without flaws.

We should acknowledge that there is good and bad in every generation. After all, it was the government leaders of Zizi's era that fanned the flames of the Cold War, suckered us into the Vietnam War, fought like hell against women's rights, labor rights, equal rights, and environmental protection. These were also the folks who worked to popularize pesticide-dependent agriculture, and their policies killed off the family farm in favor of factory farming. They're the ones who brought to market TV dinners, fast foods, and processed foods. They destroyed our once magnificent mass transportation system of trolleys and trains and paved over the country with asphalt. Their "urban renewal" scheme permitted the destruction of nearly every historic city in America, their Levittown suburbs that destroyed the concept of neighborhoods, and their shopping mall developments that have killed off so many downtowns.

As a first-wave baby boomer, it is difficult to defend the actions of my generation as well, since we have become a parody of almost everything we once claimed to hate. Boomers complained about environmental destruction and went on to popularize gas-guzzling SUVs and built minimonster homes that gobble up energy to heat and cool. It's not only the environment that we're not saving. The boomers, who once ridiculed their parents for keeping up with the Joneses, have become the greatest generation of conspicuous consumers, hold record levels of debt, and most have no savings.

While Zizi's generation cast the die for the breakup of the family, no doubt boomers brought the meaning of the words *marriage* and *commitment* to a new low. My generation scorned

Richard Nixon as a crook and a liar but gave Bill Clinton a free pass when it came to character and truthfulness.

No, there is no greatest generation. But together, with a blending of the thoughts, actions, needs, and desires of all generations, we will all help to create a better world.

Humanity Hanging
from a Cross
of Iron

Enough talking, you have to eat," Zizi said as she pushed herself up from the chair and slowly shuffled toward the refrigerator. My protests that I wasn't hungry were met by her usual "You have to eat. Look at you! You're a skinny pickle!"

I no longer tell Zizi that I exercise almost every day, watch what I eat, and really work hard at trying to stay in shape. Instead, I eat what she offers me. Besides, I would insult her if I didn't. With Italians, food is an expression of love, and for Zizi, who endures great pain to be on her feet at the hot stove, cooking is also a labor of love and it helps keep her going.

"Look what I made for you," Zizi said as she held out a bowl to show me that she had a surprise.

It was brimming with pasta and meatballs. Expending

.

great effort to walk, Zizi placed the plate in the black microwave and turned it on.

"I have to sit down a minute," Zizi said as she made her way to the table. I jumped up to help her sit, but she waved me off and slowly lowered herself into her chair.

"Are you all right? Do you need anything?" I asked.

"Would you get me a glass of water?" Zizi asked. Passing her hand over the minidrugstore of little bottles she had in front of her on the table, she sighed. "Look at all these pills they want me to take . . . what are they, crazy? If I took every one of them I'd either be a drug addict or I'd be dead."

Zizi wasn't far off. Each year about 140,000 people die from taking prescription drugs, another million are severely injured, and about 2 million are sent to the hospital.

"They're out of their minds, Jerry. Who the hell knows what happens when you take all these different pills together?"

"No one does, Zizi," I replied. "And to make matters worse, the drug companies weaseled permission from the government to leave out any warnings they don't want us to know about. Those little pamphlets with tiny print often exclude the worst side effects and most deadly reactions."

"That's disgusting," Zizi replied, with an expression of hopeless resignation.

I always get a kick out of how a single death occurring from an overdose of a natural supplement gets front-page coverage with a banner that reads something like VITAMINS CAN BE DEADLY.

Then an all-star cast of white-coated "medical authorities" are rolled out in front of the TV cameras, vowing to clamp down on potentially lethal, unregulated herbs and vitamins that "threaten the very well-being of our society and prey upon the unsuspecting." But kill off 140,000 people a year, and it hardly makes the news.

As I was telling this to Zizi, I thought of the saturated news coverage warning us of AIDS, which in 2000 killed about sixteen thousand people in the United States. I guess death from prescription drugs doesn't have the same media appeal as death from sex. Think of it: in the United States about nine times as many people die from prescription drugs each year than die of AIDS. Prescription drugs are the fourth-largest cause of death nationally—AIDS doesn't even rank in the top ten! Millions of people's lives are ruined from prescription drug *side effects*— you know, those little annoyances like brain damage, stroke, pulmonary disease, cardiac arrest, perforated ulcers, cancer, liver failure, and addiction.

Pushing the jumble of little brown plastic pill bottles off to the side, she said, "And these are only some of what they want me to take. If I got all the prescriptions filled that they give me it would cost me over three hundred dollars a month. My last prescription cost eighty-five dollars. Where the hell am I going to get eighty-five dollars?" she sighed.

Zizi has Medicare but, with few exceptions, Medicare doesn't cover the cost of prescription drugs, which is the single largest health care expense for the elderly. Because most governments prohibit drug companies from price gouging, some of the medicines she was taking cost about 70 percent less in other countries. In the United States, where drugmakers spend well over $100 million a year lobbying Washington, they essentially write the laws, can charge what they want, and basically get away with murder.

I got up and gave her a kiss. "Don't worry, Zizi, it will all work out, you can always count on me to help out," I said.

How much more time on earth does she have left? I thought to myself. The last days of her life and she, like so many others, has to worry about having enough money to pay a miserable $85 for medicine that could stand between comfort or misery, and even life and death.

No one is for wasteful social program funding or unnecessary welfare payouts. But I am an advocate of giving help to fellow humans in our society—the handicapped, the homeless, the poor, the elderly, and the mentally frail who can't help themselves. And as a researcher, I am very aware of the swelling tide of souls who fill these descriptions. They are not faceless abstract numbers and boring government statistics. Some of them are my best friends. And all you have to do is look at the declining services and financial pittance given to the average American in need to understand that all men are *not* created equal.

On the very day that Zizi was telling me of her prescription drug woes, Congress appropriated $15 billion for emergency military action in Yugoslavia. The money was taken out of the Social Security trust fund.

Then Congress added another $5 billion for "star wars"—the money pit that has already gobbled up $130 billion for a flawed protective missile shield.

It's hard to understand. Whether in peace or war, good times or bad, the military gets the financial fuel it asks for. But when it comes to a "people emergency," it treats its own as though we are bums and beggars on the dole.

To help offset the extra military spending, Congress announced a $26 billion reduction in spending, with the lion's share of the cuts coming from people's programs: education, job training, housing, health, human services, environment, parks, medical research, and veterans.

Is something wrong with this picture?

President Dwight D. Eisenhower thought so, and warned the nation, as he left office in 1960, that if the trend continued, it would cost each of us dearly:

Every gun that is made, every warship launched, every rocket fired signifies in the final sense a theft from those who hunger and are not fed, those who are cold and not clothed. The world in arms is not spending money alone. It's spending the sweat of laborers, the genius of scientists, the hopes of its children. This is not a way of life at all in

*any true sense. Under the cloud of threatening war, it is
humanity hanging from a cross of iron.*

Believe it or not, this warning cry that the military industrial complex was holding Americans hostage came from
arguably one of the greatest generals of the twentieth century.
This was no "pinko commie," as people of that era who ques-
tioned military expenditures were called. No, this was *the* general who led the United States and its allies to victory in
World War II and then served as president for two terms, a
man who ranked as both Supreme Allied Commander and
Commander in Chief. A man who really knew what it looked
like inside the military and at the top of Capitol Hill.

Eisenhower was right, but who heard him? Over $13 tril-
lion was spent fighting the Cold War from 1950 to 1990. This
is one reason why Americans are working longer and harder
than ever before. With today's military budget at the Cold War
average, the two-income family is a necessity rather than a
choice. Rightly or wrongly, there will always be a rationale to
increase arms spending. But it's simple economics and simple
choices: You cut up the pie and choose either to expand the
military or feed the people—more bombers or more butter . . .
money for health or for military hardware. Something's got to
give.

When I got married in 1972, I didn't have a job, but my
wife was a secretary making $10,000 a year with full medical

benefits. We were paying $115 (utilities included!) for a three-room apartment in a beautiful building on the Hudson River. In fact, we were even able to save money. Those were the last days of an era when a single income was enough to live well and not sink into debt. But the economic toll of satisfying a ravenous military and fighting the Vietnam War had begun to sap the economic vitality of our country. The numbers speak for themselves. As Ike said, ". . . the sweat of laborers, the genius of scientists, the hopes of its children . . ." went to the military. Federal Reserve data shows that the average net worth for 40 percent of U.S. families has declined 36 percent since 1983! And we're getting poorer. In 2000 the net worth of U.S. households fell for the first time since the government began keeping statistics in 1945.

Having taken her medication, a rested and reenergized Zizi was up off the chair, motoring around the kitchen at shuffle speed. As she was busily rummaging through the refrigerator, I asked her why it was like this.

Turning away from the refrigerator and looking over her shoulder to answer me, she said, "I really don't know the answer, Jerry, but you'll go wacky if you keep trying to make sense out of all the crazy things the government does."

The microwave *binged*.

"I'll get it, Zizi, sit down," I said as I started to get up.

"No, you sit down—you're my guest. I got it," she said, using a kitchen towel to handle the hot plate. The pasta in the dish was her own homemade cavatelli and meatballs. Zizi's face glowed as she said, "Guess what else I made for you, Honeyboy?"

"Chicken cutlets," I guessed, hoping I was right. I love the way she prepares these lightly breaded treats. She once gave me her recipe so I could try them at home:

Zizi's Chicken Cutlets

Serves 4

1 ¼ *pounds chicken cutlets, sliced ⅛ inch thick*

2 *large eggs, beaten*

1 ½ *cups seasoned bread crumbs*

½ *cup olive oil and ½ stick butter*

Wash the cutlets and dry well.

Lightly pound the cutlet slices with the flat side of a big butcher knife to make them thinner. Dip them in the beaten eggs, and press the slices into the bread crumbs, patting on both sides to make as many crumbs stick as possible. Repeat: dip them back into the eggs and then back into the bread crumbs, patting on both sides.

Heat the olive oil and butter in a thick skillet over medium heat. Add the cutlets and sauté, turning them over once after the first side is golden brown. When both sides are done, remove, salt lightly, and drain on paper towels.

"You can have some now," she said, putting the steaming plate of pasta in front of me on a paper-towel place mat. Next to it was a plastic Tupperware bowl of grated Romano cheese. Heading back to the refrigerator, Zizi pulled out a big platter stacked with chicken cutlets. "I made enough for you to take home," she said. "I also have some extra cavatelli and meatballs for you and some zucchini the way you like it, with tomato, garlic, and basil. And," she continued, reaching deep into the overstuffed refrigerator as if to pull a rabbit out of a hat, "I got you some fresh ricotta for your cavatelli. I know how you love to mix it with your macaroni."

With the large container of ricotta in one hand, braced against her chest, she slowly bent over to open the vegetable bin and, as if by magic, came out with a can of beer. "I hid this so no one else would drink it," she said.

How kind Zizi is to me. As I looked down at the meatballs and inhaled the aroma of Zizi's sauce, I plopped a couple of tablespoons of ricotta on top of the cavatelli, the way I did when I was a kid. "Thanks to you I can still have some of the tastes and smells of my past alive today!"

Just Wait Until Your Father Gets Home

Zizi reached out for the aluminum walker that seemed to be waiting obediently at the foot of the table. Grasping it with both hands, she hunched her weight forward and began a slow stroll with her wheeled companion. "I have to get something in my bedroom," she said. "Eat, I'll be right back."

While they really didn't look alike and their temperaments were different, Zizi has a way about her that reminds me of my mother, and like Mom, she's also a spectacular cook. I remember how my buddies at the University of Charleston in West Virginia would love to give me a ride home to Yonkers during breaks because my mother would have a small banquet ready for all of us after the long drive.

My favorite dish was fusilli and ricotta. Mom used to serve

the long, curly pasta with ricotta that was rich and creamy, not like the dry, pasty stuff you buy in supermarkets today. Back then, fresh ricotta came in two-pound tins that were punched with tiny holes, to let the water drain. The overflowing crown of ricotta that pushed over the top of the tin was held intact by a piece of waxed paper that was tightly fastened to the can by thick rubber bands. Proudly emblazoned on the waxed paper was the family name of the hometown cheesemaker. In Yonkers, it was Brunetto's.

What really made my mom's pasta so great was her rich tomato sauce. She'd make the sauce, or "gravy" as we called it, with sautéed veal, pork, braciole (stuffed flank steaks), some sausage, and whatever other pieces of meat "looked good" to her when she went to see Uncle Al, the butcher. Of course, her meatballs added to the richness and flavor, especially when she made them in the summer with just a touch of fresh mint.

On Sunday mornings, when we'd come home from children's mass, Mom would have a plate of little meatballs sitting on the stove waiting for us. I would do almost anything to relive those family Sundays—and to taste one of Mom's beautifully browned and perfectly seasoned meatballs.

My mother didn't go to church very often—she was always so busy cooking, taking care of the house and seven children—but my father, Lou, never missed a Sunday and neither did any of the kids. In those days, going to church was a formal affair—suit and tie, dresses and hats. Dad's ritual at mass was always the same. Ten minutes into the service he would go on automatic pilot—stand, kneel, and sit—while in a deep sleep! Whoever sat next to him in church was responsible for waking him up when he started to snore. And boy was he loud! From one end of the church to the other, Louie's snores would soar above the Latin liturgy.

The stares from the annoyed congregation would embarrass me a bit. But I really dreaded the dirty look I'd get from Dad when I'd give him a nudge to wake him up. After the service, on the way home he'd say with a straight face, "Stop poking me when I'm deep in prayer."

Going to church was worth it as long as it meant going home to freshly made little brown meatballs. They were brown because after Mom sautéed them, she didn't keep them cooking with the other meats in the sauce. That would make them mushy. She would only add them to the sauce after it was cooked. And the reason they were little was that they were only a treat. Mom didn't want us to spoil our appetites for our big early-afternoon family dinner.

After eating a few meatballs, our next favorite activity was to dunk a piece of crusty Italian bread into the simmering pot of sauce. We were told not to put the bread directly into the pot, but to spoon out the sauce and pour it onto the bread. We never followed that order because, as any true dunker knows, it tastes better when you dunk direct. Besides, even if one of us got caught with the lid in one hand and a slice of sauce-soaked

Italian bread in the other, the worst possible punishment was a mild scolding.

My parents seldom exerted stiff punishment. With seven children, four girls and three boys (I was number five), you'd think that they would have lost it from time to time, but that was rarely the case. Louie was a laid-back guy, and my mother pretty much rolled with the flow. We used to hear a lot of "Wait till your father gets home!" from Mom when we misbehaved. But bless her soul, rather than give us a well-deserved *mazzata*, or walloping, Mom, in typical Italian fashion, would bite the side of her hand.

When I was about five years old, and lived in the Bronx, my parents packed up my brothers, Anthony and Bobby, who were four and two years older than me, in their 1948 Hudson and drove us to a place that was surrounded by a high, spiked, wrought-iron fence. My father pulled up to the massive gate, turned off the ignition, looked over his shoulder at the three of us in the backseat, and sternly announced that because we were fighting so much and driving my mother crazy, they'd decided to put us in reform school to straighten us out. Oh, did we start crying! Without saying another word, Pop got out of the car and walked up to the security guard while we went into a panic, promising our mother that "we'd be good," begging her not to put us away. Dad came back to the car, stuck his head in the window, and told us to get out. He said that the guard was waiting for us to arrive. But even as the sobbing intensified and the tears streamed down our cheeks, my father said that all our crying wouldn't do any good because it was too late to turn back now that we were here. We'd been given plenty of warning to be good, he said, but we didn't listen and now we had to pay the price . . . reform school. My brothers and I promised my parents the world. We'd do anything they wanted, we wouldn't fight with each other ever again, we'd help out more around the house, and we'd behave forever.

"Let's give them one more chance, Louie," my mother said.

Half protesting, my father agreed. Of course, after a few days, life went on pretty much the way it had before. In later years they'd threaten to send us to military school, which for Bronx-born boys was like saying we'd be sent to jail. And, for the record, that menacing gate of the "reform school"? It was an entrance to the New York Botanical Garden.

On a typical Sunday, with seven of us kids squeezed around the kitchen table, we'd have a huge platter of pasta, usually ziti, rigatoni, or fusilli, with ricotta or my father's favorite, mezzani, along with the huge platter of the assorted meats that had been steeping in the sauce for hours. That was followed by some type of roast and vegetables.

We all had our places. My father, naturally, was at the head of the table. My oldest brother, Anthony, sat to his left, then Bobby and me. My two little sisters, Marie-Elaine and Nikki, sat next to each other, across from my father at the other end of the table.

My mother sat to my father's right, then my sisters Yvonne (the oldest) and Grace sat across from us boys because that was the side of the table closest to the stove, and the women were in charge of the food. Sunday-afternoon meals would last for about an hour and a half. There always seemed to be something to talk about. There was never a rush to go out and play with our friends. Being with the family, eating and talking, was enough to fully satisfy us.

I can't remember a time that a blowup at the table was bad enough to provoke our parents to send us to our room. Sure, there were squabbles, but no nasty fights. Most of our time together was spent eating, laughing, and listening a lot to my father. He was a great storyteller and could make the dullest topic exciting. Could he tell a tall tale! "Stop, Louie," Mom would say as my father started to *really* stretch the yarn that he'd been spinning. He'd give her a smile and continue on.

On Sunday nights, we'd have hot open-faced sandwiches made from the leftover roast. Dad would expertly carve the meat into thin slices and my mom would place it on freshly made toast, then smother it with the gravy she'd made from the juices of the roast.

The leftover sauce from Sunday's dinner was enough to make another meal for the entire family later in the week. So, Thursday became Ronzoni spaghetti day in our house. Because my dad was a plain pasta man, the more fancy dishes like ravioli and lasagna were usually reserved for Easter, Thanksgiving, and Christmas.

Italian tradition has it that after the parents are deceased, the brothers and sisters celebrate the holidays with the oldest member of the family. After my grandparents died, my aunts, uncles, and cousins from my mother's side, about twenty-five in all, would come to our house for most of the holidays, because my mom was the oldest. Holidays were always a carnival of fun with a cast of characters that brought out the best in life. Uncle Frank Vigilante loved to do Charlie Chaplin routines and would dress up as Santa Claus at Christmas. Tall and dapper, he had a full head of wavy black hair, a handsome mustache, and a nose that ranked in size somewhere between Jimmy Durante's and Cyrano de Bergerac's. He was married to my mother's sister Viola. They tried to have children but couldn't, so they both treated all us kids just a little extra special.

Then there was Uncle Mario with his two little mutts, Peppy and Fifi. Lean and muscular, like a welterweight prize-fighter, Uncle Mario sported one of those pencil-thin mustaches that you saw in the 1930s movies. During the Christmas season he would dress up Peppy as Santa and Fifi as a little elf. One of the attractions at his fish store in Flushing, Queens, was to have Peppy push a baby carriage, with Fifi inside, up and down the street outside the store. When I got old enough to drive, I would take my friends to see the dogs. Uncle Mario would sit Peppy down at a little wooden piano and sing "O

Sole Mio" in the dog's ear while Peppy banged out the song on the piano and howl the tune. "Peppy, go find my cigarettes," Uncle Mario would command. The little mutt would leap straight up, going from counter to counter, until he found the package of Lucky Strikes. Once he'd located them, he'd snag them in his mouth and bring them to Uncle Mario.

Uncle Al, Zizi's husband, was a wanna-be opera singer who would, from out of nowhere and out of tune, belt out one of his Neapolitan favorites with all the flair of Caruso. At the drop of a hat, the entire group of uncles and aunts would sing, dance, and clown around. Rarely was there an argument, conflict, hurt feelings, or business talk at the table. Holidays were meant to be celebrated, and no one broke that rule.

Holiday meals began at around one in the afternoon and

The Great Peppy

went on until about ten at night. Of course, the pasta was only a part of the feast. A huge antipasto and homemade soup preceded it. Then, after the lasagna or ravioli with meatballs, sausages, and a variety of meats, the obligatory turkey or fresh ham dinner, compliments of Zizi and Uncle Al's butcher shop, followed. All this was accompanied by a nonstop flow of beer, liquor, wine, and soda.

Sometime in the late afternoon, after the main course, all the kids would take off, usually outside, to play. Some of the men would take a nap and others would play pinochle. The women would be busy straightening up the table, washing the dishes, and congregating in the kitchen. About two hours later, on cue and without notice, everyone would start to migrate back to their places at the table for dessert. That, in and of itself, was another feast. Depending on the holiday, there was always a wide variety of homemade, baked seasonal specialties and an assortment of Italian pastries that each family bought from their favorite neighborhood pastry shop. It was a never-ending table full of pastries, chocolates, pies, cookies, cakes, and nuts that was finally topped off with strong espresso coffee laced with anisette.

It was a different time in a different world. And it would pass under the weight of many influences. Unfortunately, Peppy found those packs of Lucky Strikes all too often—Uncle Mario died of lung cancer when he was still in his early sixties. And poor Aunt Viola. She was only forty-one when a leg operation that went wrong forced the doctors to amputate. From there she went downhill, and two years later died from circulatory complications. Uncle Frankie had open-heart surgery and died several years later.

But there were much broader forces of change at work. Suburban sprawl stretched out the family roots. Just as my parents had moved us to Yonkers, away from my grandparents who lived in the Bronx, to find a better life, my married brothers and sisters were also moving to new places. Out of sight and out of mind, the feeling of family closeness faded as the distances grew greater.

By the late 1960s the impact of the radical social movement and a redefinition of the concept of family had started to erase many traditions that once bound us together. The "Me" generation put its personal needs and desires ahead of parental wishes and demands. Newlyweds had new ideas about family and obligations. Others moved far and wide to take jobs. I took one in Chicago in 1973 and stayed for six years. One sister moved to Florida to work, and another to China.

And as the old-timers died, the ways of life that they brought to America from the Old World eventually died with them. These turn-of-the-century immigrants and their children were able to keep alive the customs of the homeland. But by the time my generation came of age, the traces of our roots had begun to vanish. The old neighborhoods were gone, marrying someone from a different nationality became common, and the embracing of pop culture and the American way of life further diluted our heritage.

Something Is Lost
and Cannot Be
Found

The squeaky wheels of her walker grew louder as Zizi approached the kitchen. I was thinking about how the family life I so cherished had been dealt a fatal blow on Good Friday, April 9, 1971.

That year, Good Friday fell on Passover. My two little sisters and my mother always celebrated Passover with our neighbors, Irv and Ann Singer. At that time, Zizi worked as a florist at S. Klein's department store on Central Avenue in Yonkers. Each year my mother would go to Klein's and buy a bouquet of flowers to take to the Singers, knowing that Zizi would make an especially beautiful arrangement. "Flowers are God's smiling faces," Zizi once said. "If I was healthy enough today I'd still be working with them."

One of Zizi's favorite floral arrangements, which she originated in 1954, was a rosary fashioned by using little rosebuds as the beads and roses to make the cross. The rosary is a big part of Zizi's life. She says the prayer every night, and when she wakes up in the morning, with the rosary still firmly in her hands, she says it again. "If I die in my sleep, they'll find me with the rosary in my hands," Zizi told me.

On this Passover my mother had called Zizi to tell her she wasn't feeling well and would be sending one of my sisters to pick up the flowers. But at the last minute, for some reason, she changed her mind.

"It was around three in the afternoon, Gerald, when I looked up from the counter where I was working and saw your mother and sister walking toward me," Zizi told me. "I'll never forget, your mother was wearing a blue coat with a fur collar. God bless

My parents, Louis and Marie

her, she was always dolled up and always looked dignified. She even cooked and cleaned in a dress and low-heeled shoes.

" 'Marie, you came,' I said. 'I thought you were going to send one of the children.'

" 'I was going to send one of the girls but I had to see you, Sis,' your mother said to me. 'But please hurry, Phyllis, I'm very tired. And please make a bouquet for Bobby, he loves flowers,' she said." My brother Bobby had just gotten married, and my mother wanted to get the newlyweds a little something special as well.

"The Easter/Passover holiday was very busy for me," Zizi continued, "so I didn't have time to talk to her much, other than to tell her how happy and surprised I was to see her. I immediately started to put the arrangements together and remember walking out from behind the counter to get some more flowers when I looked up and saw your mother sitting in a chair against a backdrop of hundreds of Easter lilies. I'll never forget how she looked sitting there with all those flowers behind her." She paused. "Your mother and sister left a few minutes later after I had kissed them good-bye. I had told her I'd talk to her tomorrow."

Zizi went back to the counter and about fifteen minutes later she noticed a lot of commotion outside the store. One of her co-workers went out to see what was going on and told Zizi that there must have been an accident because there were an ambulance and police cars around the scene.

"I went about doing my work, not giving it another thought. But when I got home a few hours later I found out that it wasn't an accident," Zizi recalled. "It was your mother—she'd had a massive heart attack and died right outside the store, just after she got into the car with your sister. Marie had come to see me before she died. I lost the best friend I ever had."

I was twenty-four years old and living in Queens when my mom died. Luckily, I had visited her only two days earlier. My sense of humor was very different then—I was the clown of the family, and that day I had her laughing so hard that she was pleading with me to stop. The youngest child for several years,

Me

until my two sisters were born, I was "the baby" of the family and always close to my mother.

My brothers and sisters say that I was Mom's pet. Maybe I was because she meant the world to me and when I got the telephone call that she had died I felt like the world had ended. I remember waking up the next morning hoping that it was just a terrible nightmare. Zizi says that when you love too much you hurt too much. I know what she means.

My brothers, sisters, father, and I sorrowfully ate Easter dinner two days later with a banquet that was fit for a king and made by a queen. From soup to nuts, my mother had been cooking and baking all week to make sure that everything had been prepared for the holiday. As my grandmother would say, *Quando la casa preparata, la morta se presenta,* when the house is all prepared, death presents itself.

It is said that when a mother dies, the family often dies with her. With Mom gone, our big house that had been filled with so much life and so many people for so many years quickly became cold and empty. Dad either lacked the energy or didn't have what it took to keep the spirit alive. My mother proved to be the glue that held us all together and no one could, or tried, to fill her shoes.

Actually, for a variety of reasons—mostly squabbles, petty jealousies, bruised egos, and an unwillingness to forgive and forget—our family had begun splintering even before Mom's passing. "Brothers and sisters should love each other," she'd say, "they shouldn't fight." I still wonder whether it was a broken heart from seeing what was happening to her once loving family, or a heart attack, that took my mom when she was only fifty-seven.

Without her to repair the short circuits and blowups between brothers and sisters, sisters-in-law and brothers-in-law, our once tightly knit family began to disconnect and for the most part we went our separate ways. I've tried my best to mend fences. From time to time, when Pop was still alive, we'd all get together for family celebrations. But despite the best efforts and finest intentions, the family flame hardly flickered.

Pop died ten years after Mom. He never remarried. "I'll never find another woman like your mother," he had told me a few years before he passed on. And just as I feel about Mom, I thank God for blessing me with a dad like Louie.

My ex-wife and I had always tried to keep the holiday spirit alive by cooking and baking the traditional specialties our parents made. And for several years after Pop was gone we'd share holidays with a few of my brothers and sisters. Now when the holidays roll around, I not only experience the loneliness and sadness of my broken marriage, I also feel a deep emptiness from the loss of a family life that I know will never return.

Zizi has taught me to understand that there's a sad story in everyone's life. When we look at someone we don't know—a person on the street, a personality in the media, or a business acquaintance we just met—we see and judge them as we would judge a book by its cover. Unaware of the story of their lives, we know nothing of the pain in their hearts or the troubles that they shoulder.

It may be true for most of us, but speaking for myself, it seemed that I only had to look outside my doorstep, to our neighbors, the Singers, to learn some of the important lessons of life.

Mr. and Mrs. Singer were like family, and they were regulars at our holiday celebrations, parties, and cookouts. Ann was short and plump with brightly tinted blond hair and red, red lips. Like my mom, she was always dressed up, always wearing high heels, and always so loving and sweet. Irv Singer was more the sporty type. He was "casual cool" before it was hip. Medium height, strong, and relaxed, Irv Singer was a handsome man with a boyish smile. He had a way about him that made me think he could make friends with anybody—and he probably did.

Looking at Irv and Ann, no one would have known the pain that lived in their hearts. The Singers lost their son Myron when he was a teenager. Although he was a few years older than me and more my brother Bobby's friend than mine, we often played together. A warm sweet guy, Myron was sturdily built, a great swimmer and a strong athlete. Tragically, and mysteriously, he drowned while away at college in his freshman year. The Singers appeared to shoulder Myron's loss without bitterness. But every time his name came up, I could see in their faces how deeply his death affected them. Unfortunately, tragedy would again strike their household.

As a kid, I would often hear the huge electric double door of their garage open up at around 6:30 in the morning as Mr. and Mrs. Singer left for work. In those days few people went to work as early as they do today. In my house things didn't get stirring until around 7:00 A.M. Imagine, my father raised seven children comfortably, without my mother having to work, and without him having to get up and get out of the house by 5:30 A.M. as is now so common.

Mr. and Mrs. Singer could be classified among the category of hard workers that has now become the norm. They left the house early and didn't get back home until around 7:00 or so at night from the fabricating business they owned, Able Steel, in Long Island City. Sundays were their only real day off, and quite often they would stop in at one of our many family gatherings for some good food, a few drinks, and some small talk.

But their routine of life abruptly ended in the early 1980s. Mr. Singer was forced to stop working when he was diagnosed with lung cancer. I was sitting with him one day, as he was resting in the sunroom of their beautiful home, and Mrs. Singer was busy in the kitchen. A heavy cigar smoker, Mr. Singer always had a raspy voice with a great South Philly accent. Despite the age gap between us, we got along like pals and would talk a lot about many different things, from sports to finance to women. Only in his sixties, Mr. Singer was rapidly deteriorating. I used to visit often and try to cheer him up, thanking him for all the kindness he'd always shown.

At one time he loved to tell jokes and was always "up." But he wasn't like that anymore. "Gerald," he said to me now, his voice low. "I'm very angry. I worked hard all my life, I made a lot of money, and I was always so careful not to spend it carelessly. Life wasn't supposed to end like this for me." Tears fell from his eyes.

I didn't know what to say. I'd never seen him like this before. "Mr. Singer," I finally pleaded, "don't say that. It's not good for you to feel like this now. You had a great life, a wonderful wife, and raised fine children. You've made a lot of people happy . . . you gave a lot."

He smiled wistfully and held my hand with both of his. "It's true. I am bitter. I played by the rules and in the end I was cheated. I'm not ready to die. I don't want to die. I worked like a slave all my life only to end up like this, without really enjoying all that I worked for. For what? For money? Why did I do this to myself? It wasn't supposed to end like this," he repeated.

What he was saying struck me as the truth and there was nothing I could say. Having known Mr. Singer for some twenty years, I knew it wasn't in his soul to sell his life for work and money. Somewhere along the way, as with so many of us, he changed course and set his sails to reach financial success first, believing that he would live happily ever after.

Mr. Singer's regrets and his untimely death were among

those life lessons that I grasped but didn't fully understand as they were being taught. Young and naïve, I believed those kinds of things only happened to other people . . . not me. As I get older the painfully truthful words and the tragic image of Mr. Singer stay with me. I have really tried my best to live my life to the fullest. When I sense that I'm squandering it, I flash back to the life and death of Irv Singer to help me create a more fulfilling future.

I wish more people could have known, seen, and heard him speak in those final days. Because, looking at the dominant work/money ethic today, I can see that a lot of people will be bitter tomorrow when they are shocked into realizing that they didn't live before they died.

People have always worked hard, but life in America wasn't nearly as hectic as it is today. When I was a kid, the word "stress" wasn't a part of my vocabulary. We didn't have to be at school until 9:00. Now many are at their desks as early as 7:00 A.M. and then go home with thirty pounds of books strapped to their backs—so they can keep busy with homework. Why, I even remember something called "banker's hours," which meant that bankers only worked from about 10:00 A.M. to 4:00 P.M. each day. In fact, most people only worked nine-to-five jobs because they could afford to work less, buy more, and live better than we can now in many ways. Without the burden of heavy work that people have on them these days, families back then had time to be families. It was tough enough to hold things together during those family-value years of generations gone by. Given the prevailing pressure cooker conditions, it's a miracle that there aren't even more fractured families.

Indeed, 24/7 has replaced 9 to 5 when describing our work habits. Companies like FedEx brag that they deliver on Sundays "because the world works seven days a week." Some people call this progress. I question the sanity of it all. However, one thing can't be denied. The vast majority of people are working longer and losing economic ground. Americans are working approximately 160 more hours a year now than 20 years ago. And with the exception of some recent minor upticks, real wages for 75 percent of U.S. workers fell every year since 1987, according to the Bureau of Labor Statistics.

During his trip to Mexico in 1999, Pope John Paul II may have summed up the problem when he said, "In more and more countries a new system prevails based on a purely economic conception of man—this system considers profit and the law of the market as its only parameters."

At times I wonder if it is Zizi's Old World cooking that brings back so many old-time memories.

I was startled when Zizi's hand gently stroked my head. "I didn't hear you coming," I said.

Whenever I eat at Zizi's, she rarely eats with me. She's always making something or getting something. It was like that with my mother. I hardly remember her sitting down to enjoy the fruits of her labor. As with Zizi, her enjoyment came from nourishing family and friends.

Zizi reached into one of the two big pockets of her dress and handed me a little brass medallion. "This was Grandma's when she was a young girl, Honeyboy. She gave it to me and now I want you to have it." The trapezoid-shaped medal with Florentine etching held a small round picture of Saint Anthony enclosed in glass and on the other side a picture of the Immaculate Conception with *Ricordo*, Memory, inscribed in the metal. For Neapolitans, Saint Anthony ranks right up there at the top of the saint list and has the honor of being the Patron Saint of Lost and Found. When something precious is missing, Catholics often say, "Saint Anthony, please come around, something is lost and cannot be found."

Zizi tells me that in life there are givers and takers. Whether it's cooking for me or giving me a cherished memento, she tries to reciprocate and never wants to feel like she's taking charity when I help her out financially.

I went to get my key chain from the bedroom so I could attach the treasured medallion. Showing Zizi what I had done with her gift, she told me to always carry it, because the spirit of Grandma would always be with me.

When I use my keys, I often rub the medallion between my fingers and think of the symbols that it holds and the loved ones it connects me to. And, as Zizi said, it *is* a good-luck piece—not for superstitious reasons, but to remind me of my good fortune to have been born into my family. Now that I have Grandma's medal inscribed with *Ricordo*, it helps remind me of those many memories.

"Life goes speeding by. Pay attention to what I have to say . . . let this sink in. Live today as if it's your last day," Zizi counseled.

As I absorbed Zizi's wise words, fully aware that there was a lot of room for personal improvement, I washed the dishes—under her protest—and told her I had to be on my way. It was getting late and the weather was changing. I wasn't looking forward to the long drive back home in the rain. "Sorry, no Scrabble tonight," I said as I started to collect my coat, keys, and the care package of goodies that Zizi had waiting for me.

We hugged and kissed good-bye, and as always she insisted on escorting me to the front door.

"Drive safely and please call me when you get home. . . . I'll worry if you don't" were Zizi's last words as I closed the door behind me.

Make Money Your God and It Will Plague You Like the Devil

Only a few days had passed since I had last seen Zizi when I unexpectedly found myself back in Manhattan on business. "Oh, what a surprise," she said when I telephoned to tell her I'd be arriving around 10 P.M. "I get to see you twice in one week!"

When I got to Zizi's house, I had to ring the bell several times and pound on the front door before she finally heard me. "I'm coming, I'm coming," I heard her say. On my toes, peering through the small window at the top of the door, I could see her in her blue-and-white housedress, smiling as she tried to hurry to greet me. Zizi unlocked the door, showered me with a flurry of hugs and loud kisses, and in the very next breath insisted I eat, because in her way of thinking I had to, regardless of the time of day and whether or not I was hungry.

Hand in hand we slowly headed toward the kitchen. I sat down in my usual chair at the table, where there was a peppers-and-egg sandwich waiting for me. Neatly enclosed in plastic wrap, the sandwich sat on a plate alongside a glass and a can of beer atop the usual paper-towel place mat. She had prepared the sandwich earlier in the evening, so by now the savory egg frittata of hot and sweet Italian peppers, garlic, and Parmesan cheese had soaked its way into the Italian bread. (Zizi makes a mean peppers-and-egg sandwich, but nobody comes close to matching the way Aunt Viola made them. She called me "the Peppers-and-Eggs Kid," because I'd always hound her to make them.)

Zizi asked me why I was in the city. I was doing some radio and TV interviews, and I told Zizi of a telephone call I had gotten earlier in the day from ABC's *20/20*, about a story they were putting together on the roaring stock market and the enormous amount of money investors were making.

The program was going to compare the lifestyles of the late-twentieth-century rich with those of the late-nineteenth-century's Gilded Age—a sardonic name coined by Mark Twain to describe the excesses of the wealthy class and the rampant corruption in politics and business that went with it. They wanted to know if the new rich today were more likely to keep a lower profile than the money-flaunters of the past, quietly splurging at home with fine meals and good friends.

In a word, no. A casino fever had gripped the nation, and the word on Wall Street and trumpeted by the media was that "you had to be in it to win it." Fortunes were being made overnight by stock speculators, and anyone like myself, pointing out that the dot-com bubble would soon burst, was dismissed as a gloom-and-doomer. The signs of extravagance were everywhere. The Land Rovers, the lines at Cartier, the waiting list at Jean-Georges, the outrageous executive bonuses, the trophy homes—they all added up to an ostentatious display of newfound wealth. Day in and day out, the magnificent money machine of the late 1990s created an enormous new monied class that splurged on fine wines, puffed on fat cigars, and spent millions to hire big-name performers for private weddings and celebrity chefs for personal dinners.

"You don't go out so you can't see what's going on, Zizi," I said, referring to omnipresent displays of self-centered grandiosity. "On trains, in planes, on the street, in the elevator, restaurants, and even the bathrooms, you can't escape the noise of cell phones and big shots bragging about their big deals."

Zizi replied, "Money talks and it never bores people. And don't forget," she continued, "I lived during the Roaring Twenties and the Great Depression. I don't have to go out, I've seen it all before."

The producer for *20/20* told me that she had already shot a segment with a small group of Wall Street types in a fancy

Manhattan restaurant, who began the evening with a $1,000 bottle of wine and then drank a $5,000 bottle before dinner was over. Similar stories passed on from New York City restaurateurs involve financiers who close a big deal, launch an IPO, or make the right market play and drop $20,000 on dinner.

"It's obscene," Zizi said, shaking her head. "When money becomes the god that people worship, they lose sight of what's really important in life. In my lifetime I've seen a lot of people show off when they get too big or brag when they strike it rich, but it's a lot different today. Before there was a belief that if you were on the top it was a privilege that brought with it responsibilities. Now it's everyone for themselves."

I told Zizi that it wasn't as though billionaires are bad and the rest of us are good. The greater problem is another troubling trend seen among a large group of 24/7 workers who brag that their purpose in life is to work hard, work long, and make a lot of money. They are so wrapped up in their jobs that they have little knowledge of life beyond their work. Outside their individual entertainment and hobby interests, if the topic had nothing to do with high technology, the financial markets, or making money, the chances are it's unlikely to generate much notice among them. We have become a society that is so busy making money and "deferring" life with a hope of reaching financial nirvana that we have little time and energy left to focus on much else. We have become a society afflicted by "affluenza," the money disease.

In 1999, expectations were so overblown, that polls show 75 percent of college students expect to become millionaires! Many Generation X'ers who had hoped to cash in on the Internet boom flaunted their ninety-hour workweeks and vacationless years as a badge of honor. They're not alone. Eighty percent of workers of baby-boomer age consider themselves workaholics. These martyrs for money tallied up their consecutive days at work as though it were a challenge to Joe DiMaggio's fifty-six-game hitting streak.

"These kids just don't know any better," said Zizi as she sipped a cold cup of coffee. "They're only doing what is being taught to them. A wise man should have money in his head, not in his heart. You come into this world with nothing and go out with nothing. All you take with you is your honor, dignity, and good name. And if you don't have a good name, then they'll say, 'I'm glad he dropped dead.'"

I often hear philanthropic tightwads cop a plea that they'll give their billions back to society "before they die." While big bucks can breed big egos, I have to wonder if they are so out of touch with life and so filled with themselves that they actually believe they can determine when their time is up. Or are these cash hoarders so smart that they know something about life and death that Irv Singer—or John F. Kennedy Jr.—didn't?

In the latter half of 1997, I was asked to talk to the staff of *The View* about trends. One of the subjects I discussed was the near-global outpouring of grief and sympathy over the recent tragic death of Princess Di. The princess was seen by many as a person of great wealth and childlike vulnerability who really connected with everyday people and wanted to improve the lives of those less fortunate. Many believed that Diana cared for them and she was seen as irreplaceable.

Who can we turn to now for the inspiration that could be found in her strengths and weaknesses—vulnerability, compassion, power, and prestige? Which world leader, which athlete or religious leader is revered and truly believed to be politically neutral and unconditionally concerned for *all* people's spiritual health and personal welfare? By coincidence or cosmic design, one candidate in the running would have been Mother Teresa, and she died just one week after the princess.

With her folded arms resting on the table, Zizi leaned toward me and said, "Gerald, people are confused. In their hearts they know something is very wrong with life today, but they can't put their finger on it."

"You're right, Zizi," I said. I mentioned a 1999 poll that was conducted by the Pew Research Center for the People and the Press. Pew concluded that "people think the American way, politically and economically, is a remarkable achievement and it does work." But when you've looked behind the numbers and analyzed the depth and meaning of the questions asked, you could see they measured "achievement" by the thickness of our wallets. The poll also found that technological and material success is undercut by the 70 percent who said the nation suffered from a "moral breakdown." The Associated Press summed up the results with observations from people they interviewed about the poll: "There's more money, but less human caring," said one. Another said, "Life may have gotten better, but people haven't gotten better." A poll conducted for *U.S. News & World Report* drew a similar conclusion, showing that some 90 percent of Americans consider "incivility" a big problem.

These are astounding findings that should have made headline news but were hardly reported. All the pieces fit together neatly—road rage, air rage, student violence, broken families, corruption, crumbling morals—but people discard these quality-of-life facts and instead embrace the standard-of-living dogma as *the* measurement of success. "Life in this country has gotten better," stated another person the AP interviewed, citing the strong economy, the Internet, and the so-called Information Age as proof.

If the "American way" was working so well, why was "stress" cited as the primary cause for the 25 percent increase in sick days? Why do stress-related problems account for 60 percent to 90 percent of doctors' visits in the United States? How come 25 percent of employees are angry at work? If "life has gotten better," why are 5 percent of our children being fed Ritalin to calm them down, and why are we gulping down more than a million dollars' worth of Prozac a day to keep steady? In the year 2000, a depressed America spent $10.5 billion on antidepressants. Growing at an annual clip of 20 percent, it's the best-selling category of prescription drugs. The nation's inner turmoil is so intense that almost one-third of all Americans say they've been on the verge of a nervous breakdown.

If the facts show—and the people say—they're unhappy and morally starved, and large numbers are on the verge of cracking up, is the "American way" delivering on its promise? When the media and politicians talk about other nations that don't have the financial and material riches of the United States, they tell us the people in those countries are "living in poverty." But as any seasoned world traveler will tell you, "poverty" is a relative term. It can be argued that while people living in poor nations lack our material comforts, many of them possess the wealth of community and the family prosperity that has dissipated in America and among her people. Although America is wealthy financially, emotionally she is deep in debt, without a surplus in sight.

"I feel sorry for people today and I'm sad to see what's happening to our country," Zizi replied, after absorbing all this. "I hope they wake up before it's too late. The Bible warns us not to worship the golden calf." She sat back comfortably, with her arms still folded and resting on the table. "They think they'll find the yellow brick road paved with gold and that will lead them to happiness. I'm glad I'm old and won't be around for too long because it will get a lot worse."

Then, pausing to search her memory, Zizi quoted Henry

Fielding: " 'Make money your God and it will plague you like the devil.' " And then came her favorite Ben Franklin quote: " 'Money never made a man happy yet, nor will it. There is nothing in its nature to produce happiness.'

"I think people would be happier if they followed the old rule to make as much as you can, spend as much as you can, and give as much as you can," Zizi said.

Work to Live, Don't Live to Work

At eighty-three, Zizi always amazes me with her instant recall. She can often rattle off quotes, repeat the entire lyrics of songs, poems, and sayings that go back to when she was a little girl. "How do you remember all this stuff, Zizi?" I asked.

Pausing for just a moment, her eyes twinkling, and in a voice mimicking a young girl, she repeated a verse that she remembered singing on the ship that carried her, my mother, and my grandparents from Italy to America when she was five years old:

So iccino e so carina
So la gioa di Papa

Si me sporca la vestina

Mio Papa mi vatira

Vo saperno come va

Pee Pa, Pee Pa

(I am a little dear and I am loved

I am my father's joy

If I soil my dress

My dad will spank me

Would you like to know how?

Pee Pa, Pee Pa [two tiny pats on the cheek])

The Church of San Pellegrino Matire in Altavilla Irpina, Italy,
opposite the street where Zizi was born

It was 1919, and Grandpa, like so many other turn-of-the-century European immigrants, came to America to find his fortune. They lived on East 117th Street in Manhattan in an area that was mostly Italian and where many friends and family had already settled. And, as in the villages they came from, all the aunts and uncles lived within a few blocks of one another. My great-grandparents wanted no part of the New World, so they stayed behind. Grandpa would go back from time to time to visit, but Zizi never did. I made a pilgrimage a few years ago to my dad's town of Vico Equense, which sits on the sea just north of Sorrento, as well as to Mom's rugged village. Pop's town is not much of a tourist attraction, but among Italians from the region it's known for a restaurant that sells "pizza by the metre." The folks from Altavilla Irpina, where my mother and Zizi came from, were more friendly and told me that I had the eyes and face of many of the people there.

For Zizi and my mom, Italian Harlem must have seemed like Italy. Each Sunday, when they were little girls, they would go from building to building and round up the younger cousins to go to mass.

"Your grandma would give me a nickel to light a candle to Saint Anthony and a penny to put into the collection basket," Zizi told me. "On the way to church we'd pass a man with a pushcart selling hot waffles for a penny each, and one Sunday my little cousins started to cry that they wanted one. There were six of them so I bought them each a waffle. When I went home Grandma asked me if I lit the candle and I turned red like a beet. She took my little hand and gave it a smack. I started to cry and told her what had happened. She gave me a hug, and so help me, that's the only time she ever hit me.

"Every Sunday, after church—but before lunch—the paesanos would make the rounds to say hello and have a drink. In those days, after a hard workweek, Sunday was the day of rest. It was more than just a day of rest and respect for the Sabbath, it was a day for the family.

"Do you remember those times?" Zizi asked.

"Sure, Zizi," I said, thinking back to when I was a teenager. Up until the mid-1960s, only the candy store, drugstore, and bakeries were open on Sunday.

People went to the candy store for newspapers, cigarettes, and maybe a cup of coffee and a hard roll. I reminded Zizi that I was a soda jerk at Urich's candy store in North Yonkers. Urich's was right across the street from Christ the King Church, and would close about 1:30 in the afternoon—a half hour after the 12:00 mass was finished.

Working for Harold Urich and Herbie Strauss was one of the best jobs I've ever had in my life. When I was growing up, I couldn't wait to turn sixteen so I could get a job there. The perfect odd couple, these two cigar-smoking brothers-in-law, Harold and Herbie, were characters from a lost era. Harold was tall and a bit portly, while Herbie was short and thin. Harold smoked big fat cigars, Herbie smoked little thin ones. Harold was a worrier, Herbie never worried. Harold used to watch his money, and we would tease him about always counting the "coo" (Harold's nickname for money). Herbie was a big spender who would let the good times roll and go first class when he traveled. Harold always kept the soda jerks busy cleaning up the store when there weren't any customers, which was why all the guys liked to work during easygoing Herbie's shift.

But I liked working with Harold. My father trained me to be a hard worker, so compared to what I was used to, Harold was a piece of cake. Dad owned a beautiful yacht-and-cabana club on the Hudson River in the late 1950s and early '60s, and I worked there every summer until I was sixteen. My job began at eight in the morning and I'd work until the evening, doing everything from emptying garbage bins, scraping barnacles from the bottoms of docks, gassing up boats, cleaning cabanas, mowing lawns, working the snack bar, and always painting something— bottoms of boats, docks, or buildings. Whenever I complained about working too hard or not getting paid enough, Dad would say, "You call this work? It's a *vacation*. Kids from the city would do anything to trade places with you." It was a family business, and I felt good helping out.

In the nearly three years I worked for them, I never heard Harold and Herbie argue. They truly loved each other, and would tell me so. We laughed like hell and joked around every chance we'd get. Working for these two beautiful men was a complete joy. And although I was only making $1.15 an hour, the benefits were exceptional. All my friends from high school and the neighborhood would hang out at the soda fountain after school. Urich's was also where I met my first true love, Carole, a real sweetheart of a girl who to this day fills my heart with wonderful memories. We dated for about four years, but we were both too young and I did not appreciate just how special she was. I remember my dad would look at me and say, "Son, did you ever hear the expression that youth is wasted on the young? Well, they were talking about you!" I understand now what he meant.

Theresa and Gerald's first Communion

Actually, Carole was my second true love. Theresa was my first.

Catholics receive their first Communion at seven years old because we're told that's when we reach the age of reason. I don't agree with a lot of things the church says, but I'm with them on this one. I knew I had reached the age of reason because the only thing important to me was kissing Theresa as we sat in the last row at religious instruction. If I were a kid doing that today, I'd be expelled, arrested, or sued for breaking the underage smooching law or brought up on charges of sexual harassment. But as you can see from the photo, we were in love. How my heart broke when Theresa moved away a few years later. I never saw her again.

"Gerald, are you listening to me?" Zizi asked.

"No, did you say something?" I replied in a daze. "I was thinking of my life a long time ago." I told Zizi about Theresa.

"That reminds me of the story about two little children in school who were just like you and Theresa," Zizi said. "The little girl raised her hand and asked the teacher, 'Can I have a baby?' 'No,' the teacher said. The little boy sitting next to her leaned over and said, 'You see, I told you not to worry.'"

I get a kick from just watching Zizi tell a joke. She always cracks me up.

"Good, I made you laugh," she said. "Each time you laugh it adds years to your life."

I thanked her for the extra years. Then she continued to tell me how America's changing work habits have affected our family values.

"Like it or not," she said, "when people weren't working on Sunday the family was together. Are people so blind that they can't see what has happened? The family is breaking down because the family is hardly together. People work all the time."

"I guess you could say parents have been forced to bond with business and not their babies," I replied.

"How times have changed," Zizi said, shaking her head.

"Not only were people free on Sunday before the seven-day workweek became routine," I said, "but if you worked Saturdays it was for only a half-day. My European friends tell me they 'work to live,' but Americans 'live to work.'" The facts bear them out. Today's work pressures are so intense, and demands so great, that 82 percent of executives even work on their vacations. We put in the longest hours among workers in industrialized countries and work 350 hours more per year (almost nine full workweeks) than Europeans.

"Maybe workaholism should be treated like other forms of addiction," I said. "Workaholics, like alcoholics, make everyone around them miserable and their addictive behavior and abuse trickles down to family, friends, and co-workers."

A backlash is building against this trend of working so hard that you don't have time to enjoy the pleasures of life, and it's being championed by people who practice "voluntary simplicity." Previously trapped on the treadmill of work hard, consume heavily, and acquire big debt, these down-spenders want to check out of their hectic lifestyles. Now satisfied with what they have, their mission statement is to pay off debt, moderate consumption habits, work less, and live more.

Because for all the hard work, what have we really gained? In 1970, 36 percent of households had dual wage earners; today, it's more than 60 percent. And that old Ozzie and Harriet model is history: marriages with the male as the sole breadwinner fell from 51 percent back in 1970 to 26 percent in 1997. When I was a kid, only a handful of the moms in my neighborhood worked full-time. By 1970, the year I finished graduate school, some 30 percent of women with children younger than a year old worked, compared with nearly 60 percent today.

Where is the progress? With moms and dads now working, finances have not really improved. According to the Census Bureau, median family income is almost 3 percent below the 1989 level and the child poverty rate grew by 15 percent from 1979 to 1998! The bureau also reports that eight million Americans in families earning more than $45,000 a year had trouble paying rent, medical bills, or other basic daily needs. Some fifty million people overall had trouble paying for mortgages, food, utilities—you know, those little things in life.

At the same time, more Americans are saving less. Savings were no longer important we'd been told, because almost 50 percent of American households were invested in the stock market. But that's not accumulated wealth, ready to be used in case of an emergency. And now as the high-flying stocks have tanked, so has the bankroll. In 2000, for the first time in the twenty-year history of the 401(k) retirement savings plan, the average account lost money! Back in the 1970s, the U.S. savings rate was around 10 percent. Today, it's about *minus* 1.5 percent—a level not seen since the early days of the Depression.

As I mentioned some of these statistics to Zizi, it was clear she really wasn't very interested in hearing them.

Uncrossing her arms and with a dismissive wave, she said, "Jerry, I know about family life. I don't need to add up a bunch of numbers to know that it's gotten a lot worse.

"I remember when they began to sell us on 'quality time.' The 'experts' said it was okay *not* to be around your children during the day, or when they came home from school, or when they're growing up. Instead, they tried to convince us that it wasn't the amount of time spent together but the *quality* of that time. Baloney! When a child needs you they need you. Not a stranger, or baby-sitter—"

"Or nanny," I interjected.

Zizi pushed on. "No day-care baby-sitter is going to give a child the same love and nurturing as a parent," she said. "I've raised four children, your mother raised seven, and we were always there for you kids."

I told Zizi that today it's common for children as young as six weeks old to spend ten or more hours a day in day-care centers. And the trend will continue as real-income levels for the majority of workers drop, and as more single mothers have children. For example, the majority of first births—someone's first child—were being born to women who were unmarried.

"People like to brag about how much time they spend at work and how hard they work," Zizi continued. "We'd have a much more compassionate country if people bragged about how much time they spent with their children."

I rattled off other statistics indicating that 90 percent of adults believe the lack of adult supervision of children is a cause of violence. And today about one-third of all children in the United States, an estimated five million between ages five and thirteen, are on their own while parents are at work.

"That's exactly what I mean, Gerald. People know what's going on. But they feel trapped. Once my generation leaves this earth you won't have many parents who think like this anymore, but I have a suggestion. If one of the parents doesn't have to work—be it husband or wife—they should stay home to raise their kids. And, please, Jerry, don't quote those reports showing that it doesn't make a difference if a child is raised by strangers . . . that's just nonsense."

Zizi was referring to a study in the news indicating that children of women who work outside the home suffer no permanent harm because of their mother's absence.

"I feel sorry for the parents who are forced to work long and hard just to make ends meet," Zizi said. "It's not all their fault and they're not who I'm talking about. Not everyone has a choice and it doesn't mean that a child can't be raised to be a fine adult if the parents aren't there all the time. But it doesn't have to be as bad as it is.

"I may be old, but I'm not ignorant and I'm not stupid. I know what's going on. America is the richest country in the world and there's plenty to go around. If the crooked politicians and business cheats weren't stealing so much from us, doing big deals with their friends, and pilfering the wealth of our nation, life would be easier and we'd all be better off. I know the way life used to be and I know the way it is today. People are so busy running here and there and working all day long that they have little time to know what's really going on right under their noses. Plain and simple, they're being robbed blind.

"And people are digging their own grave," she added. "They just think about buying, buying, and buying. They think they can shop their way to happiness by filling up their lives with *stuff*," she said, waving both arms, ". . . so they spend their way into a financial hole and have to work all the time to climb out."

This got me thinking. Realistically, how can most Americans find time to understand the scope and extent of the deals being made between politicians and their benefactors when they're so busy working and struggling to hold families together? After dealing with the problems of a long business day, the kids, the marriage, the bills, et cetera, how many people want to hear about the serious problems of the world? Overworked, with sore feet and a backache, who wants to hear about hundreds of billions of dollars in corporate welfare that's siphoned from "little people" programs and the "little people's" paychecks? Each year legislative giveaways, subsidies, tax breaks, and bailouts are doled out to enrich telecommunications giants; defense industry monopolies; Wall Street tycoons; banking powers; television and entertainment moguls; mining, logging, and oil interests—and virtually every other industry and profession that fills the campaign coffers of elected officials and the two ruling political parties.

The following headlines tell the story. But most people missed them because they are usually reported on the inside pages of newspapers, and then buried in the journalistic boondocks. Here are a few classics:

MINING LAWS CHEAT TAXPAYERS

CRUISE LINES REAP PROFIT FROM FAVORS
IN LAW

IRS AIDES TESTIFY CORPORATIONS GET
SPECIAL DEALS

BIG BREAKS FOR BIG COMPANIES A TREND

U.S. BOWS TO BUSINESS ON FOREIGN-TAX
LOOPHOLE

FEW REAL WINNERS WHEN STATES FIGHT
FOR BUSINESS

Even in the most robust of economic times, with corporate profits reaching a record $4.5 trillion in 1998, the government routinely withdraws hundreds of billions of dollars directly from working people's paychecks and deposits them into the bank accounts of some of the richest people in the world and into special corporate interests.

Headline-hungry politicians rail and the media saturate the airwaves with stories about welfare queens, the homeless addicts, and others at the bottom of the social barrel who rip off the system to buy Cadillacs, or booze, or to get high. Here's one big-time scam you probably missed if you blinked an eye because it went virtually unreported by the biggest mouths and the toughest talking heads of TV news. Rather than auction off or sell the remaining broadcast spectrum, politicians gave the television networks—Disney's ABC, General Electric's NBC, and Viacom's CBS—about $100 billion worth of publicly owned airwaves for free!

From Sears Roebuck, the Gap, General Motors, AT&T, Boeing, Bechtel, Intel, Mercedes-Benz (now Daimler-Chrysler), to building subsidized playpens—called football and baseball stadiums—a broad range of scams, disguised as deals, are always justified under the banner IT WILL CREATE JOBS. But study after study confirms that the jobs that are created end up costing the taxpayers more than they're worth, often pay poorly, are temporary, and the only real beneficiaries are the corporate welfare recipients.

The sports industry is one of the biggest culprits on the public dole. In addition to the twenty new publicly financed major-league sports parks now in the works, there are scores of minor-league teams on the take. But the public is often misinformed of these scams by journalistic gymnastics. For example, *The New York Times* ran this headline heralding the return of minor-league baseball to Newark, New Jersey: IN NEWARK, A CARNIVAL AS THE BEARS RETURN. In this quarter-page puff piece, the use of the word "Carnival" in the headline set the tone for the reader to view the new stadium as a positive development before reading the details of the article. The story goes on to say that the 6,000-seat, $34 million stadium was financed "by the city and Essex County." Cities and counties don't produce products or provide services that generate revenues. They collect taxes. Therefore, it really wasn't "financed" by them but by *us*. More accurately, the story should have said that city and county politicians, without permission or consent, picked the people's pockets to finance this business deal for a small group of friends and speculators.

Indeed, so strong is billionaire power and influence peddling in America that even when the electorate votes projects down, politicians overrule the people's voice and levy new taxes to finance the deals. For example, voters in Seattle had turned down a proposition that would give $370 million of their money to some of the richest men in the world, including Microsoft co-founder billionaire Paul Allen, who wanted a new stadium for his Seattle Mariners baseball team. Ignoring the will of the people, the legislature pushed through a tax levy anyway. Adding insult to injury, the billionaire owners asked for another $100 million from the working stiffs to pay for cost overruns.

A once avid Yankee fan, Zizi remembers the days of Gehrig, Ruth, and DiMaggio. Although there were money squabbles back then, and without union representation many players were shortchanged, there was still a different spirit to the game of baseball. "I love to watch the game but I can't stand some of those prima donna players who always want more money or those crybaby owners who keep raising prices," Zizi said. "I became a Mets fan in their early days because they were a real hometown team. But now they're a money team like the rest of them so I don't watch as much as I used to."

"Will it ever change?" I asked.

"What do *you* think, Honeyboy? You're the trend man!" she said, throwing the question back at me as she slowly pushed herself up from her chair.

I've thought about this a lot over the years. "Yes, it will change," I said. "But each of us has to improve our inner world first for the outer world to change. That's what the quest for 'spirituality' is about."

"That's very nice," she said, bursting my New Age bubble. "I just hope you're right. Because if we stay on the path we're on now it will only lead to more misery." Zizi worked her way slowly to the counter. "Look what else I made for you," she said, calling my attention to the Ziploc bag filled with Italian anise cookies dangling from her hand. One thing Zizi had over my mother was her anise cookies. They're so light and flavorful, and I love to dunk them in my coffee. These aren't biscotti in the traditional sense, mind you. They're white cookies, about three inches long, braided in a twist, roughly two perfect bites. Whenever Zizi makes some, I share them with the folks at work. My assistant, Judy, asked Zizi for the recipe because she loves them so much.

Zizi's Anise Cookies

8 eggs

1 (1 ounce) bottle anise extract

7 teaspoons baking powder

¾ cup olive oil

2 cups sugar

6½ cups flour

Preheat the oven to 375 degrees.

Mix all the ingredients together until they form a soft dough.

Break off a piece about the size of a walnut, and roll into a rope about 5 inches long. Fold in half and gently twist. Continue until all the dough is used.

Place the cookies on a lightly greased cookie sheet. Bake on the middle rack, about 15 minutes, until golden brown. Makes 12 dozen.

"Zizi, please stop! You know me, I have no willpower and I'm really trying to lose weight."

"Lose? You need to gain some weight," Zizi said, lowering herself into her chair across from where I sat at the small table.

"My pants are too tight and I don't want to buy a new wardrobe, so I have to lose weight." I told her that at five feet eight, I'm not a big guy, so a few extra pounds show up on me as excess baggage. To make my point, I squeezed the love handles hanging over the waist of my slacks.

As with most of the first wave of baby boomers, I've learned that losing weight is a lot harder now than it was just a few years ago. Before, if I cut back on a bagel for breakfast and ice cream after dinner, I'd be back to the weight I wanted in a week. Today, even without the bagel and sweets, not only do I not lose weight, but I actually gain more on top of the excess.

"Please," I tried once more in protest, "I can't."

"Yes, you will. Don't insult me. I made it for you," Zizi replied matter-of-factly. "Besides, I don't know how much longer I'll be cooking and baking, so you better enjoy it now." She had a good point. The hell with my diet. Once Zizi passes on, I'll never have these tastes and smells to enjoy again.

"You're right, Zizi, I'll eat some now and take the rest with me tomorrow." It was getting late and it had begun to rain. In my younger years it seemed as though I could drive forever, but the hour-and-a-half trip to rural Rhinebeck was just too much for me to handle on this night.

"Tomorrow? You mean you're going to stay overnight?" she said, with the enthusiastic delight I used to feel when one of my aunts or uncles would stay the night at our house when I was little. "I'm so happy. The only time I really sleep soundly is when you sleep over . . . that's when I feel safe."

I planted a soft kiss on each cheek. "Thanks for another great meal, Zizi, but now we have to move on to more important matters." Zizi nodded in agreement. She knew what I was talking about.

I walked through the small archway that separates the kitchen counter from the refrigerator, and into the dining room. I turned to my left, knowing it would be in its usual place—lying on the floor under the window in the worn, oversized white shopping bag. Zizi was already poised for action when I returned. I placed the bag on the empty chair next to me and then, one at a time, I pulled out the pieces and placed them on the kitchen table. First, the large plastic board mounted on a swivel, then the two blue plastic holders and the zippered pouch that held the wooden Scrabble tiles.

"You beat me the last time, Zizi, so I pick first."

A Useless Life
Is an Early Death

Zizi never knew what hit her. She was doing what she had been doing for the past fifty years—playing bingo at Mount Carmel Church. Dotty, Zizi's decades-long bingo buddy, was sitting next to her when she heard Zizi make a strange gurgling sound.

"Are you all right, Phyllis?" Dotty asked. Not realizing that she'd made any noise, Zizi replied, "Of course I'm all right. Why do you ask?"

That evening, when Zizi got home from bingo, she wanted a snack, so she heated up some spaghetti. After eating only two forkfuls, she started to vomit—violently and continually. Her children told me her last words were "Please help me."

Zizi had had a brain aneurysm. The doctors said if they

operated, her chances of making it were about 2 percent. Given the seriousness of her condition, her old age, and problematic health history, if she did survive, she might be better off dead. Her family, with the doctors in agreement, chose to let nature take its course. Sitting vigil with her children, Ann, Ron, Florene, and Maria, I watched her drift in and out of a coma for two weeks. Her youngest daughter, Maria, took charge of the situation, making most of the decisions as conditions changed. A devout Catholic like her mother, Maria held out hope for Zizi, with the belief in the power of prayer.

But as time moved on, Zizi became more unresponsive and increasingly frail. As the days rolled past, we thought it would only be a matter of time.

Two weeks after her seizure, I was heading back to my office in Rhinebeck when I decided to visit a longtime friend, Paul, who owned a printing business in Yorktown. Work could wait. I hadn't seen Paul in a while and missed him. I pulled off the road and called my office to let them know my plans.

Just as I pulled into the parking space next to the loading dock of his plant, Paul trotted out to meet me. "Your office called," he said. "Your aunt is going to be operated on at ten o'clock." Zizi's family had been trying to reach me because she had taken a sudden turn for the worse and they decided an operation was her last hope.

I looked at my watch. It was 9:45. "Damn it, Paul, she's twenty minutes away in Westchester Medical Center. I gotta go. Keep in touch," I said as I backed up the car and sped south to Valhalla.

As I pulled into the massive parking lot of the medical center, I began thinking about the quickest route to Zizi's room. Somewhat familiar with the hospital's layout because of my frequent visits, I decided to bypass the elevator and raced up the three flights of stairs. When I arrived her bed was empty. I sprinted to the nurses' station to find out where she was.

"Mrs. Villane is being operated on," a nurse I had not seen during my previous visits told me.

"I know," I said. "When did she leave and where is she now?"

"They took her down about forty-five minutes ago," she said.

"Where?" I asked.

"Oh, you can't go there. I'm sorry."

Instinctively, the words flew out of my mouth. "I'm her son. I just got in from out of town and have to see her before they operate."

Suddenly more helpful, the nurse told me how to get to the operating room. "I think you're too late," she said. "Good luck."

The directions were confusing, but I thanked her, trotted down the hall, and ran down the four flights to the basement. It's kind of strange, the thoughts that run through your mind at

times like these. As I wove my way through the maze of hallways, trying to remember which left and which right to make,
I was thinking how cold and ugly the basement looked and
that it didn't seem like the appropriate place to perform brain
surgery.

Now in full trot, I rounded a corner and saw what I never
expected—a hallway filled with several gurneys of lifeless bodies. Had I made a wrong turn? Did these people die under the
knife? It was hard for me to imagine that patients waiting for
surgery would be randomly strewn around a hallway.

Cautiously I moved from gurney to gurney, afraid that I
would startle a stranger and squeamish because I didn't know if
the people were dead or alive. I finally spotted Zizi, lying with
her eyes closed. Her head had been shaved and dressed. A
sheet and light blanket covered the rest of her, leaving only
her face showing. I bent over, gently placed my hand on her
forehead, kissed her cheek, and whispered, "Zizi, it's me—your
Honeyboy."

In what seemed to be slow motion, her eyes opened
slightly—but her head and the rest of her body were frozen,
motionless. Her soft hazel eyes, dulled by the yellow-tinged
whites, rolled toward me.

For two weeks Zizi hadn't communicated with anyone and
I didn't know if she could understand me, but at that moment
I believed she could. "Listen, Zizi," I whispered into her ear.
"This is what you have to do. Whatever happens, don't fight it.

Let go. Whatever direction you're going to go, just go where it's the easiest."

Zizi had told me that when Cosmo was in the hospital, each day she would go to Saint Lucy's Church and pray at the outdoor grotto of the Blessed Virgin for him to get well. Seeing her kneeling down on the cold stone steps one day while she was praying, the parish priest, Father Ducca, came over to ask how Cosmo was progressing. Through her tears, Zizi told the priest that Cosmo wasn't getting better and that she was praying for God to please not take him away. "Over and over, I ask God, 'Why did you give me such a beautiful baby and now you want to take him back?' "

"You're praying too hard, Phyllis," Father Ducca said. "Why don't you leave it in God's hands? You don't know what the future holds for him. If your baby lives, you don't know if he will suffer in pain or how this sickness will forever affect his life. Have trust in God, Phyllis."

I didn't want Zizi to struggle to fight for life if she was ready to die. I would rather she leave in peace than die in anguish. And I didn't want her to fight for a life that would leave her critically disabled or without dignity.

She slowly looked away and closed her eyes. With tears streaming down my cheeks, I kissed her again. I told her goodbye. I said, "I love you."

Zizi pulled through the operation, but it would take many weeks before we'd know if she'd ever fully recover. From the medical center, she was transferred to Helen Hayes Hospital, just across the Hudson River from Westchester, where they specialize in rehabilitation. At first, when I would go to visit her, she'd just mumble incoherently and showed no awareness of the people in the room. I was doubtful of ever seeing the Zizi I'd always known.

After several weeks she began to speak a few words that seemed to make sense. But she would fade in and out of awareness and it would be months later before she even knew where she was or what had happened to her. Her first recollection of consciousness happened when she saw her daughter Maria standing by her bed. She noticed Maria was pregnant, and put her hand on her daughter's tummy and said, "You're going to have a beautiful little boy with big brown eyes. I saw him and I know what he will look like." When Matthew was born, it was no surprise to Zizi that he looked exactly as she had seen him in her semiconscious state.

We were all stunned by her recovery. "I'm like a cat—I have nine lives," Zizi said. "I've had blood on my brain, water on my brain, a shunt in my head, six operations, forty-five incisions on each leg, an umbilical hernia—I have been cut open from side to side and top to bottom and I'm still alive. There must be a reason."

When I think of all the spiritual guidance, moral nourishment, comfort, compassion, and emotional strength that Zizi gives to family and friends—along with the countless meals she has served them—I think I can figure out the reason she's still around. So many people are dependent on her kindness and love that they would be devastated had she not survived this health crisis. "I just want to be here for those who love me," Zizi said.

The doctors said it was a miracle that she made it. "I thought I lost you three times during the operation," the brain surgeon, Dr. Duffey, would tell Zizi later. Zizi remembers one of the times he almost lost her. She thought she'd left earth for another world.

"I was standing in a very large room and saw a lot of people that I had known who had already passed on," Zizi recalled. "It was very nice there and I felt so great," she said. "I saw your mother, Uncle Harry, my cousin Caroline, your great-aunt Fioredeva, and my brother Nicky who had died in a car accident on the same day your youngest sister was born. And everyone I saw looked like they did when they were in their thirties, the same age as Christ when he died."

Zizi also said she saw the comedian Danny Thomas and a friend of hers, Mel Miller, mingling among the departed family members. She would later learn that Danny Thomas had died the day she was operated on and Mel Miller just a few days earlier. After seeing many of the souls she had known on earth, Zizi then walked into a large hall and met a man whom she had never seen before.

" 'Hello, Phyllis,' the stranger said.

" 'How do you know my name?' I responded.

" 'I got a good report from earth,' he said.

"On the floor of the hall, not far from where I was standing, was an enormous tray of food. I remember thinking how heavy it looked, but when I bent over and picked it up it was as light as a feather. I handed the tray to the man I had just met and asked him to please feed the people. He took the tray from me and I then asked him, 'How do I get out of here?'

"He said, 'Walk through the door.'

"As I walked toward a door, I remember being so happy that I didn't have the usual pain that I always feel when I walked. I opened the door, but behind it was another door, so I opened that one too. It led to a long corridor and the end of it was a huge white light, the size of the sun, but bright white, not yellow. I walked down the corridor toward the light and then suddenly, just before I was about to reach it, I turned left and started to walk on clouds. That's the only thing I remember between the night I started to vomit until about six months later when I started to get back on my feet. I know there is another world after this one."

A few weeks after regaining consciousness, Zizi realized that twice in the morning and twice in the afternoon, she'd find herself playing Scrabble with a strange woman. Weeks turned into months and each day the woman would tell Zizi it was time to play the game. Finally, Zizi asked, "Why do you make me play Scrabble all the time?" The woman, a therapist, replied, "So I can win one game for a change!"

Zizi contends that Scrabble therapy helped get her brain going again. That's why, to this day, she loves to play it so much and why she also enjoys word-puzzle books. Whenever I'm in New York City's Penn Station I make it a point to visit a newsstand that carries a wide assortment of them and buy some for her. When I bring Zizi a new stack of puzzle books, her face lights up like a child's. It's the simple pleasures that bring her real joy. Zizi says that, like crocheting, word games and puzzles keep her mind active and that too many people her age waste away by always watching TV. "Idleness is an early death," she said. "By keeping my mind busy I don't have time to ponder my problems. Life is too precious to waste." Soon after her recovery she wrote this poem.

REASONS

Thank you God for sparing my life,
So I can go home to Alfred and be a good wife.
I came home for a reason, what could it be?
God would soon take Alfred away from me.
Now I'm all alone in my golden years.

I live with memories and shed many tears.
So, I try not to cry and keep doing my best,
because a useless life is an early death.

I woke up at 6:30 the next morning in my bed at Zizi's house, and my mind flashed back to 1991, the year Zizi had suffered the near-fatal brain aneurysm. As I lay in bed, warmth filled my heart as I realized how grateful I was to hear Zizi stirring about in the kitchen and smell the coffee she was brewing. I chuckled when I thought about the trouncing I had taken from her the night before in Scrabble—and the sly look she gave me when she laid all seven tiles down on the board *and* hit a triple word score. Since her dance with death, Zizi seemed in many ways more vibrant, her wit quicker, her thoughts sharper. How blessed I felt that she was still alive and well.

I slipped on the pair of lightweight sweatpants that I keep in her small guest bedroom, a room filled with a full-size bed, shelves of books and knickknacks, and the floor cluttered with bags of yarn. I made the bed and walked the short distance down the narrow hallway to the kitchen. I called out "Good morning, Zizi!" in a loud voice, hoping that hearing me before seeing me would keep her from becoming startled.

"Oh! Good morning, my Honeyboy," Zizi said, looking up from her crocheting. "Can I make you breakfast? Would you like some juice? An egg? Cereal?"

I kissed her on both cheeks. "Just coffee," I replied as I picked up the old-fashioned aluminum-clad percolator pot and filled the two little floral painted cups she had put on the table. "I'm still full from last night. I can't eat another thing."

"How about a doughnut?" she said, uncovering a dish filled with the same kind of little chocolate doughnuts I remember John Belushi devouring on *Saturday Night Live*. Not a bad idea, I thought. A little sugar rush might give me the push I needed. Before I finished dunking the second doughnut in my coffee, Zizi replied predictably, "That's not enough for you to eat. Can't I fix you some eggs?"

"Come on, Zizi, I polished off that huge sandwich late last night," I said, and got up from the table. I headed into the dining room to fetch the big torn white shopping bag. "And now it's time for 'A.M. Scrabble,'" I announced, using my best game-show host voice. "I can't go home until I beat you. You humiliated me last night."

Would You Rather
I Smoke Pot?

Zizi and I see eye to eye on a lot of things, but we part company when it comes to the business of making coffee. While I'm into the gourmet blends, she still brews that stuff that's *not* good to the last drop. Neither her weak cup of java nor the little chocolate doughnuts provided the jolt I needed to get out of my bleary-eyed state, so I was having a tough time focusing my mind on the Scrabble board. Stuck with two A's, two U's, two I's, and an O, I was on my way to losing another game.

"How was your night, Zizi?"

"I slept well and have been enjoying the morning, sitting outside and thinking about how good it is to be alive," she said. "A lot of people my age are tired of living and afraid to die.

Me? I'm happy when I'm feeling a *little* good without too many aches and pains. How was your night?"

"I hate to complain, but you know how it is," I replied. "Zizi, I love to visit . . . and I love sleeping over, but the smell of smoke is everywhere . . . I can't escape it," I said, moaning about my lousy night's sleep. Despite keeping the two windows of the small room wide open, I couldn't escape the smell of forty-five years of cigarette smoke that has found its way onto every object and into every crevice of Zizi's house.

"Oh, now you too! Leave me alone. You sound like Florene," she said, referring to her daughter who visits from California. "I suppose you would rather I smoke pot?"

"At least you'd get a high rather than just getting sick from inhaling those chemical sticks that you're hooked on," I said, not taking her seriously.

"You think you can get me some?" Zizi asked in a hushed tone and with a sly smile. "I always wondered what it would feel like to 'get high.' "

"What, are you kidding? Maybe if you were in better health and your brain could take the jolt," I said, laughing.

"Do you smoke pot?" she asked me.

"I smoked but didn't inhale," I said, trying to avoid the question.

"Now, now, Gerald, don't be so presidential," Zizi said, waving her finger at me, ". . . tell me the truth."

"Sure, Zizi, I smoked pot when I was younger. It was a part

of life for a lot of us kids, growing up in the sixties. But it's not something I do anymore. Besides, if you're hooked on smoking something, you're probably better off smoking marijuana than killing yourself with that crap," I said, pointing to her pack of Merits.

Zizi turned her attention back to the Scrabble game and started to rearrange the little wooden tiles on the blue plastic tray in an attempt to find a word. That was the end of our conversation about her smoking. Her children hound her to quit, but she can't. I never hassle her to stop. It's just that I hate the smell of stale smoke. But her addiction and her remark "Leave me alone" started me thinking about the whole marijuana-versus-cigarette controversy. What possible rationale is there for justifying one set of rules that permits a favored group of people to sell and promote tobacco products that kill several hundred thousand people a year, while using another set of rules to harshly punish those who sell pot, which inflicts a much lesser degree of damage? When I think of all the misery those little cancer sticks have brought to addicted smokers like Zizi and the pain to millions of families, I can't help but get disgusted at the level of duplicity coming from the U.S. government and politicians. As part of my job, I closely follow reports of tobacco companies being accused of intentionally spiking cigarettes with poisonous chemical additives to induce nicotine addiction. From the $300 billion in medical expenses it costs each year to treat smoking-related diseases, and the 450,000 smoking-related deaths per year in the United States, it's evident how successful the companies have been in hooking innocent victims on the smoking habit.

All the illegal drugs combined are inflicting a lot less damage; 5,000 Americans a year are dying from cocaine and heroin—few, if any, from marijuana. Yet 1.5 million people are arrested for drug-related crimes, and the prisons are packed with almost 450,000 drug offenders, most of them small-fry users and not the big-fish traffickers that the tough sentencing laws were created for. Almost 80 percent of all drug arrests are for possession, of which 44 percent involve marijuana.

When comparisons are made between cigarettes and drugs, we are told that cigarette companies are not breaking the law. But whose "law" is it? These laws aren't commandments or holy sacraments that have come down to us from on high. They are simply a list of rules made up by men and women who get buckets of money, from industries like tobacco and alcohol, to act as those industries' mouthpieces. Under God's law, perhaps, the makers and sellers of "legal" people-killing products may ultimately receive much stiffer sentences for their crimes of greed and murder than those now serving time on earth for selling illegal drugs.

And the federal government, after years of misguided warnings that smoking pot would lead to crack and heroin addiction, finally admitted in 1999 that it is not a "gateway drug" that leads to hard drugs. It's not even a health risk.

According to the *Merck Manual of Diagnosis and Therapy:* "There is still little evidence of biologic damage, even among relatively heavy [cannabis] users."

While I am not condoning marijuana use or denying the other effects it may have, including lethargy and motor impairment, I see a contradiction between incontrovertible fact and an insane public policy that has ruined so many people's lives by branding them criminals and throwing them in jail. On the other hand, it actually all makes perfect sense in a system in which justice is measured by the size of political campaign contributions.

Cigarette makers—seeking to minimize risk, limit liability, and eliminate potential competitive entrants into their $25-billion-a-year businesses—have given $30 million to the Democratic and Republican parties and to party candidates over the past nine years. That's why, despite the death and destruction smoking has caused, cigarette companies and their advertising agencies have been able to escape criminal punishment, while small-time perpetrators are prosecuted to the fullest . . . especially those with the darkest skin.

A major study by Human Rights Watch found that 63 percent of drug offenders doing time in jail are black, even though there are five times more white folks doing drugs.

Since 1980, American taxpayers—the "little people"—forked over more than $250 billion to fight the losing war on drugs. Add to that another $9 billion annually that goes into the pockets of the prison industrial complex that incarcerates the druggies. Yet despite the high cost to taxpayers and those doing time, marijuana usage among teens increased during the 1990s. According to the Centers for Disease Control and Prevention, 27 percent said they smoked pot in 1999.

Another example of political and judicial hypocrisy is the attitude toward alcohol, which kills about 150,000 people a year. Alcohol abuse costs society an estimated $150 billion annually. It is the leading factor in motor vehicle deaths, and it is the number one *drug* problem among teens. Approximately 25 percent of children in the United States are exposed to family alcoholism or alcohol abuse. Some 23 percent of college students are frequent binge drinkers. On and on goes the list of gory details of human suffering from alcohol abuse that takes a much higher toll on society than drug abuse.

Addictions are medical problems that can never be solved by policemen. Failing to acknowledge that Prohibition couldn't stop the flow of booze, the government kills debate and attacks the messengers who want to end the war on drugs. "Legalization is surrender to despair . . . it cannot and ought not be any topic of serious discussion to our nation's debates of the challenges of illicit drugs," proclaimed Congressman Benjamin Gilman, in a typical response to calls for drug decriminalization.

I summed up my thoughts and asked Zizi for her view.

"I agree with Ann Landers," she replied, referring to an

article she had recently read by the syndicated columnist. "People shouldn't be treated as criminals if they keep pot for their own use."

It took Zizi about an hour and a half to trounce me, but I hung around, determined to finish the game rather than get to the office on time.

As we started to clear the tiles from the board, I found myself watching how quickly Zizi's nimble little hands snatched up the letters and deposited them in the blue pouch. Before I could put the Scrabble board back into the shopping bag, Zizi had pushed herself up off her chair and was opening the screen door.

"Take your coffee, Gerald, and sit with me outside. I'm going to have a cigarette."

"You go ahead. I'm going to wash up and get ready to go."

What Do They Think—
I Was Born Yesterday?

The ritual on my way out the door is always the same. As I'm gathering things, Zizi assembles a giant care package of food. And just when I think she's done, she adds even more to the package. "Please," I plead to her with praying hands. "*Basta!*" Enough!

"How about some bread?" she urges.

"Okay," I reply. "But that's it, no more."

"I have some nice Locatelli cheese," she insists.

"Zizi, I have Locatelli, provolone, parmigiano, and yes, I have no bananas," I sing back. "Stop! Please stop," I beg on bended knee.

Even that doesn't stop her. After emptying the refrigerator, she unloads the freezer, pulling out plastic containers holding a variety of prepared meals—lentil soup, pork chops, chicken cacciatore, a frozen loaf of Italian bread, and a bunch of bagels . . . you name it, it's in there—and is heading toward the bags on the counter for me to take home.

As she packed away the chicken cutlets that I enjoy so much, she told me how meticulous she is when it comes to cleaning poultry. After trimming the cutlets of fat and gristle, she pats them down with plenty of salt and washes them thoroughly in a mixture of water and lemon juice . . . twice.

"I have to be thorough," she explained, pausing to use some old-school Italian hand language—palm up and four fingers touching the thumb while flicking her hand up and down a few times. "Just who the hell are they trying to kid?" she said. "The food today is crap. I grew up eating the best quality available, and I can tell you that the taste of the meat, the richness of the eggs, and the flavor of the fruits and vegetables of years ago were far superior to what you get today. How about some bananas? You said you have no bananas, Honeyboy," she teased. Without waiting for a reply, she put a bunch of bananas into the care package.

"And the chicken," Zizi continued, "I'll never eat chicken out, not even at a friend's house. I take extra care in cleaning it because of the way they're raised and slaughtered. It's disgusting. Your uncle Al used to sell the best meats available, blue-ribbon quality, not like most of the junk they sell today. I remember when I'd bring my godmother, Aunt Margarita, fresh meat. She would look at it and say, '*Che bella carne fresca.*' What a beautiful fresh meat. Today they fatten everything up with hormones, shoot them full of drugs, and feed them whatever they can shovel down their throats. And I'm insulted by those phony commercials about how wonderful they treat their tender chickens. What do they think—I was born yesterday? It's a disgrace what they've done to our food."

Who could argue with that? Food today not only lacks quality and flavor; eating it can be hazardous to your health. So hazardous that, according to the Centers for Disease Control and Prevention, about eighty million Americans were stricken with food-borne illnesses last year, and about nine thousand died. Yet every time there's a massive product recall or rash of food-related illness, the agri-industry "experts" and government officials tell us, "The United States has the safest food supply in the world."

"I think it was Hitler who said if you repeat the same lie often enough, people will eventually believe it" was my reply. "If our food supplies were so safe, thousands of us wouldn't be dying and millions wouldn't be getting sick. It's not as if America is the only highly advanced society and the rest of the world is like Calcutta."

The U.S. food supply is not the safest. People in other developed nations aren't being killed off or getting their stomachs pumped from *E. coli*-, *Salmonella*-, listeriosis-, and *Campylobacter*-infected foods at the rate they are here. Is it any mystery why people love to eat the foods of Italy, France, and other countries they visit? It's not only because of the way Europeans prepare the food, but also because the food itself is often of superior quality. That's one reason why the European Union erected trade barriers to restrict U.S. hormone-treated and drug-injected beef from coming into their countries (another reason is to protect their farmers from low-quality cheap imports).

Of course, the Europeans have their own food problems. The British practice of mixing sheep brains, organs, and body parts to cow feed has helped create the dreaded mad cow disease—the nightmarish condition that eats away the brains of the cow as well as those of the people who eat the infected meat. But in the main, we've become so desensitized from hearing the names of the food-borne parasites plaguing us in America that we forget how deadly and crippling they can be: *E. coli* produces fatal blood and kidney damage; *Listeria* causes bloodstream infection and meningitis; *Campylobacter* leads to paralysis that begins in the legs and spreads to the chest and neck.

And now the human strain of mad cow (bovine spongiform encephalopathy, or BSE) has crossed over from the United Kingdom to the United States. In 1998, two meat warehouse workers in Miami, Oklahoma, died of Creutzfeldt-Jakob disease (CJD), which is linked to BSE. Since then, other CJD victims have been reported in Denver. But you would have needed a magnifying glass to find these stories in the newspapers because they were scantily covered.

There's also growing concern that it may not only be Alzheimer's disease that's attacking millions of people in the United States, but CJD. We're led to believe that when people are diagnosed with or die from Alzheimer's, they were extensively tested and later autopsied. That's not the case. The diagnoses are merely guesses. Autopsies, except under rare circumstances, are no longer routinely performed in the United States.

And just as they have traced the cause of mad cow disease to the waste products, body parts, and organs fed to fatten up cattle in the United Kingdom, there is growing evidence that escalating outbreaks of food-borne illnesses in the United States are a direct result of both feeding and slaughterhouse practices.

Always pressured to cut costs, agribusiness and factory farms fatten up poultry and livestock with such culinary goodies as chicken and turkey manure, dehydrated food garbage, burned-out fat from restaurant deep fryers and grease traps, cement-kiln dust, newspapers, cardboard, hog manure, human sewage sludge, plus millions of carcasses of dogs and cats that died at the vets or were euthanized at animal shelters.

"My cows are fat as butterballs," says rancher Lamar Carter, a chicken-manure devotee. He told *U.S. News & World Report*, "If I didn't have chicken litter, I'd have to sell half my herd. Other feed's too expensive."

Agribusiness "scientists" claim there is no proof that feeding decomposed human, pig, chicken, and turkey excrement to animals poses any danger to the animals or is a health risk to humans—and the Food and Drug Administration swears to it: "Feeding manure may not be aesthetically pleasing, but it is safe if you process it properly," says the FDA's Daniel Mc-Chesney.

When I mentioned this, Zizi could hardly believe me. "When your uncle Al had his butcher shop they used to brag that the beef was corn fed. Now, it's garbage fed. I think people have lost their minds, Gerald. Don't they have any common sense? Would that same farmer who fattens up his cows with manure, decompose his own crap and eat it? Would he feed it to his children? The government man," she said, referring to McChesney, "says there's nothing wrong with eating meat raised on manure? And he's supposed to be protecting us? He should take decomposed chicken shit sandwiches to work for lunch every day, if he's so damn sure of himself. He should eat his words. We'll probably come down with new diseases years from now, and all these geniuses will be wondering how it happened."

As a researcher following mad cow disease in the United Kingdom since 1987, I remember when government ministers assured the public that "British beef can be eaten safely," while they were covering up evidence to the contrary. It took until 1995, after the numbers of mad cow victims kept growing, before the government was finally forced to admit what it had long known: if you eat mad cow meat, your brain will be eaten in turn.

I told Zizi that the numbers of people getting sick and dying from food in the United States are only rough guesses and that they are probably higher than what's being reported. The government admits that it has no reliable tracking system, and only a small fraction of people with food sickness report it. Finally, the entire budget of the Centers for Disease Control and Prevention for food safety issues and outbreak prevention is only $6.5 million.

If you think that's a bad joke, the Food and Drug Administration spends only $68 million a year on food safety to protect the health of 280 million Americans. (To put things into perspective, one B-2 bomber cost $2 billion each.)

The USDA and the FDA, like the Environmental Protection Agency, the Occupational Safety and Health Administration, and the Consumer Products Safety Commission, are fronts—Potemkin agencies. While they have big, important-sounding names, they are underfunded and have limited power to police the industries they monitor. They also serve as revolving doors for bureaucrats who take jobs as executives or lobbyists in the industries they once regulated. The door also swings open to let private-sector industry executives move into the public sector as agency directors, department heads, and other high-level regulatory positions. These foxes-in-the-chicken-coop lull us into believing they are watching out for our interests, but in practice they're the lapdogs to special interests of the industries they are supposed to police.

Although the USDA can close a food plant for violations, neither it nor the FDA can force a company to pull dangerous foods from the marketplace. And it's highly unlikely they ever will, since the food industry gave Congress some $41 million in political contributions over the past decade to protect soft regulations, according to the Washington-based Center for Public Integrity.

Indeed, a *Detroit Free Press* analysis showed the U.S. Department of Agriculture did not publicize the most serious food recalls 39 percent of the time. The reason for the secrecy, according to the USDA's deputy director, Phillip Derfler, is "to avoid needlessly damaging the reputation of food companies." Keeping to their word, the agency refused to publish the results of *Salmonella* tests that were conducted at meat and poultry plants in 1998, even though *Salmonella* is the most common bacterial cause of food-related illness.

It is estimated that 1 out of 10,000, or about 4.5 million eggs, is infected with *Salmonella* and that 71 percent of chickens bought in stores are contaminated with disease-causing bacteria. But when you look at factory-farming practices, this should come as no surprise. The egg industry routinely extends the egg-laying lives of chickens by intentionally starving them of food and depriving them of water for up to two weeks at a time. After the chickens lose all their feathers, food is restored and they can now lay bigger eggs. Bigger eggs bring bigger profit. But this process of "forced molting" also weakens the immune system of the chickens. These starving, weakened, dehydrated birds are then vulnerable to *Salmonella* bacteria, which in turn is passed on to people eating their eggs, according to researchers. Although these chicken-coop concentration camps are banned in Europe, U.S. egg industrialists defend their practice of starving chickens as "essential to maintain profitability."

To make matters worse, because our factory-farmed livestock are routinely injected with massive doses of antibiotics (nearly half of the antibiotics made in the United States are given to animals), the risk of being infected by drug-resistant *Salmonella* bacteria has increased dramatically, according to the CDC, as antibiotics are passed on through the food chain.

Zizi remembers major brands, like Sara Lee, Oscar Mayer, Hormel, and others, that recalled some 40 million pounds of processed meats and several hundred thousand gallons of dairy products feared tainted by *Listeria*. But she, like most of us, probably doesn't remember the recall of 141 tons of beef by IBP, the nation's largest beef processor, the 1.5 million pounds of hot dogs and lunch meat recalled by Winn-Dixie, or the 25 million pounds of ground beef recalled by Hudson Foods. The number of products recalled for life-threatening microbial contamination has increased almost fivefold since 1988, according to the FDA.

And Zizi's correct. It's a fact that people weren't getting food sickness years ago the way they are today. Scientists have found sharp increases in stomach illnesses and diarrhea in the United States over the past fifty years. And names like *E. coli*, *Listeria*, and mad cow weren't even a part of our vocabulary until recently.

Unable to stuff any more food into the bulging shopping bag, Zizi was searching the counter for a backup. After finding one that she thought would do the job, she turned toward me and said, "All my life I ate steaks and hamburgers medium rare. Now they put warning labels on packages of meat, poultry, and eggs, like they do on cigarettes, telling you that if you don't cook it to death it could kill you. Can you believe it? Now they even want you to cook cold cuts. They're not 'hot cuts.' It's supposed to be safe to eat them cold!

"What really annoys me," Zizi added, "is how they talk down to us by telling us to make sure we cook the meat till it turns gray. And then these happy faces warn us to make sure we thoroughly clean the countertops, cutting boards, wash our hands, and thoroughly scrub any other surface that came in contact with raw meat. Are they talking about handling radioactive waste—or food? Maybe we should wear protective clothing too."

Now Zizi was off and running. "Rather than clean up their act and provide us with food that won't make us sick, they pass the buck and shift the problems onto *us* for the way *we* handle *their* toxic food. In all my life, I would have never dreamed that preparing a meal and eating it could be dangerous."

I had to get going, and I didn't have enough time or the desire to keep pounding away at the sorry state of our nation's food affairs. *Why keep hitting Zizi over the head with all the facts*, I thought to myself. She's guided by common sense, and not the bean counters.

But I could not resist telling Zizi about the Tulane University study that was quickly hushed up and forced to be retracted, after it was attacked by food-industry executives and discredited by their trade associations as inconclusive and unnecessarily alarming. The Tulane study concluded that the combinations of pesticides we ingest, some of which have been linked to breast cancer and birth defects, are up to one thousand times more potent when combined with other pesticides. Even pesticides thought to be benign when ingested separately become highly deadly when combined, severely compromising our immune systems.

Pretending to be the announcer on one of those get-rich-quick TV infomercials, I stood up and said to Zizi, "Do you want to rub elbows with the movers and shakers of the country? Walk the halls of Congress, hire hookers, sleep in the

White House, and get sensitive insiders information and special privileges? Well, you can! Just send $29.99 to Lobbying 101 and learn how to Divert, Deny, and Obscure."

Zizi laughed at my joke and little routine, but by the expression on her face I could see she was saddened by the painful truth that goes like this:

LOBBYING 101
DIVERT, DENY, AND OBSCURE
How to become the perfect industry spokesperson

STEP 1. Say you haven't read the report so you "can't comment at this time." This tactic buys time. You read the report but know that if you withhold comment, within a day or two the media will move on to something else.

STEP 2. If you have no choice and are forced to make a comment on the report, say, "There aren't enough data to draw a sound scientific conclusion."

STEP 3. Claim that the findings are inconclusive, and admonish those who issued the report for "an unnecessary attempt to scare the public."

STEP 4. If you admit that you have seen the report, question the "risk standard" and attack the data as "flawed," "incomplete," or "outdated."

STEP 5. Even when cornered by scientific evidence, mountains of data, and irrefutable conclusions, you should say with a straight face, "More studies are needed to verify the theory." No matter how much the odds are stacked against you, you can always get off the hook by repeating, "More studies are needed."

"Gerald, don't people care?" Zizi asked as she packed the second bag to full capacity.

"Sure, a lot of people are wising up," I said. "That's why the health food store business is growing by leaps and bounds. But the smart money is missing a 'maxi-trend' that's right in front of us. It's Healthy Fast-Food restaurants. And it will be one of the hottest business opportunities of the twenty-first century."

No, these won't be Tofu Huts or Tempeh Burger Hamlets. You won't get the same strange-smelling food served at your local health food store lunch counter, by people who look a lot more unhealthy than those working at Burger King or McDonald's. These will be places along the road where you'll be able to stop to get a free-range, organic chicken sandwich—or a hamburger that you *can* eat medium rare. Poultry and beef that come from animals that were naturally grazed, slaughtered in the most humane manner possible, and brought to market in the most sanitary way. At one of these new, twenty-first-century eat-on-the-go restaurants, you will be able to treat yourself and your children to fruit drinks and vegetables that are pesticide free and organically grown—or milk shakes and ice cream made from hormone-free milk.

I told Zizi that this is part of what I call the "clean food trend"—one I try to practice myself. Clean food is free of all contaminants and genetic manipulation. Clean foods are processed, packaged, transported, and stored to retain maximum nutritional value, and are brought to market under the most sanitary conditions.

I'm not a fanatic. When I'm a guest, I eat what's served. When I'm on the road, I try to do my best to eat healthy. When given the choice, I try to fill my body with the highest-quality foods available. From breakfast cereals to dairy and produce, most of what I eat and drink at home wears the organic label.

I believe that a large minority—some 25 to 30 percent of the population—shares my desire for the clean organic option when eating out. But as strange as it is, there are only a handful of healthy fast-food shops scattered across the country.

If you look at the success of food chains like Whole Foods, Wild Oats, and Bread and Circus, you can understand why the organic produce market has grown about 20 percent a year over the past six years. If you've tasted the high-quality products that people are now embracing as they begin turning their backs on the old-name, lower-quality national brands that once dominated the shelves, then you'll be an investor in the Healthy Fast-Food restaurants that will someday dot America's landscape.

It took two trips to the car to carry out all the goodies Zizi gave me. "I know I shouldn't ask you this, I know it's selfish, but when will you be able to visit me again?" Zizi asked as we said good-bye.

"Hopefully next week," I said, walking slowly alongside Zizi, who was using my arm for support as we headed toward the front door. "I'll be back to beat you at Scrabble."

"Ha," she chuckled.

Lowering the car window as I backed out of the driveway, I blew a kiss to Zizi as she waved to me from behind the half-closed screen door. "Drive safely, Honeyboy. I love you. Thanks for coming," she called out.

"I love you, Zizi. Thanks for everything," I said as she began to close the door. I was leaving just in time for Zizi to go back into the kitchen, light up a cigarette, and then turn on the TV to watch the morning mass.

·

They Must Think
We're *All* Morons

"J erry, is that you?"

It was mid-June, about 7:00 P.M., and I had just arrived at Zizi's from Rhinebeck. I could hear the TV blaring as I approached the house.

"It's me, Zizi," I called out as she unlocked the screen door to let me in. After a flurry of kisses I reached for the TV remote, which lay on the kitchen table, and lowered the volume.

Zizi sat down at her usual place at the table and half sheepishly put out the cigarette that was smoldering on the pewter ashtray. "It's okay, you can turn the damn thing off. I've seen enough," she said, referring to the pictures of convoys of refugees filling the TV screen.

The Kosovo/Serbian war had recently ended—and would fade from the public's mind as quickly as it had entered. It took just seventy-eight days for Serbia, a country the size of Kentucky with a gross domestic product about one-sixth as big, to cry uncle to an Uncle Sam–led NATO.

Despite the dropping of an assortment of 23,000 cluster bombs, cruise missiles, and uranium depleted shells onto Serb military targets and Yugoslav civilians, most of President Clinton's, NATO's, and the State Department's stated objectives for going to war were *not* met:

- Slobodan Milosevic, dubbed the "Butcher of Belgrade" and "another Hitler," remained in power . . . and would do so for the next two years.
- Contrary to NATO promises and despite later claims, the Yugoslav army remained intact and was virtually unscathed.
- Control of Kosovo was taken from the grip of a group of fascists and handed over to what U.S. special Balkan envoy Robert Gelbard branded "without question a terrorist group"—the Kosovo Liberation Army.
- "Ethnically cleansed" Serb civilians replaced ethnically cleansed Albanians, as nearly 200,000 Serbs were forced from their ancestral homeland by the K.L.A. and their sympathizers.

But with the little war over and victory proclaimed, an eerie quiet settled across the United States. Just as there was no congressional debate as to why the United States should have intervened in the Serb civil war in the first place, there was a national unwillingness to analyze or debate the war's outcome. The war atrocity tables had turned, and revenge ruled. Serbs were routinely killed, their women raped, their homes torched, and their churches desecrated and destroyed. All the self-righteous politicians and policy wonks suddenly became mutes. Pro-war editorial page cheerleaders avoided comment on the subject and papered over their hard-line stand. The biggest mouths in broadcasting were clamped shut.

"All this bombing and misery and what was accomplished?" Zizi asked. Without waiting for me to reply, she gave her answer. "I'll tell you what it accomplished. They substituted one set of crooks and thieves for another."

I had made a special trip from Rhinebeck this evening because I hadn't seen Zizi in about two weeks. I spotted a Ziploc bag of her anise cookies lying on the table; my willpower melted. I sat down across from her at my usual place, pulled out a cream-colored cookie from the bag, and began to nibble away.

"Who won what?" Zizi asked me. "And what's this 'peace' they keep talking about? Mark my words, Gerald, that place will explode into war again. I don't believe a thing these politicians tell us."

About two weeks later, on July 1, 1999, Zizi's doubts would be confirmed in a bold headline that spread across the front page of *USA Today:* KOSOVO'S PLIGHT EXAGGERATED. The first paragraph of the story read:

Many of the figures used by the Clinton administration and NATO to describe the wartime plight of Albanians in Kosovo now appear greatly exaggerated . . .

which prompted *USA Today* to ask

Then why exaggerate? "In order to justify this thing, they needed to tap that memory . . . of the Holocaust," says Andrew Bacevich, professor of International Relations at Boston University.

Most of the nation was in the Fourth-of-July-weekend state of mind, and missed this onetime news report that detailed the extent to which our government lied about facts and "greatly exaggerated" the truth in order to build public support for war.

"Stop eating those cookies, you'll spoil your appetite," Zizi commanded as she went to the refrigerator. "I made you a little something for dinner." Although I had asked her not to make anything, and she promised she wouldn't, Zizi had made pork chops, green beans, and mashed potatoes. Pork isn't a part of my regular diet, but I like the way Zizi cooks the chops in a hot vinegar-pepper sauce. "I'm sorry I don't have a beer for you," Zizi said, explaining that she had forgotten to ask her daughter Ann to buy beer when she went shopping for her a few days earlier.

"Oh, Zizi, there's no need to apologize," I replied, telling her that I'd be happy with a glass of water, but not the chlorine-tainted Yonkers water. I had a bottle in my car filled with water from my well.

When I returned to the kitchen, Zizi wasn't there, but she had already put the plate of food in the microwave and begun to warm it up.

I sat down at the table and began to think about what she had said just a few weeks earlier about the war in Kosovo as we watched it being played out on TV. "Look at what the hell is going on," Zizi had said, pointing to the footage of Yugoslavia and its bombed-out buildings, destroyed bridges, and dead bodies.

"Our president says he wants peace in one breath and then gives the order to bomb women and children," Zizi said. "People who love God don't act like this. When you have love in your heart, you have God in your heart."

Zizi's eyes welled with tears as painful images filled the screen. A hysterical woman with a lifeless baby cradled in her arms. Men searching smoldering rubble where a house once stood. A little boy with a bloody bandage over his eyes wandering in shock among peasant women crying in frantic grief—victims of purported "smart bombs" and "surgical strikes."

"Zizi, it's a terrible situation," I replied. "But didn't something have to be done?"

"Yes, something needed to be done," she said, wearily. "But this? What sense does it make? It's uncivilized. These are ordinary people like you and me. They haven't done anything to deserve this. There has to be a better way. The leaders should fight it out between themselves, man to man, and leave us out of it," Zizi said firmly.

Not a bad idea, I thought to myself. A world-leader death match, a fight to the finish. It certainly would simplify matters. "Nah, forget it, Zizi," I said. "I read that Clinton refuses to even *talk* to Milosevic, and you want them to go at each other in battle?"

"I don't understand," she said, clearly confused by my comment. "How could this be? They *need* to negotiate for the sake of the people. God gave us life. We're not supposed to take it away."

Reaching out to me from across the table, Zizi extended her hand and repeated a ritual that's performed among congregations at mass around the world. "Peace be with you, Gerald," she said in a soft voice as her warm hand gently clasped mine.

"Peace be with you," I replied with a smile and a nod.

Zizi got me thinking. Why wouldn't our president speak with their president? What was the big deal? Why had it become such a radical diplomatic concept to negotiate leader to leader just as John F. Kennedy and Nikita Khrushchev did to defuse the Cuban missile crisis? Maybe it was because Kennedy and Khrushchev each knew how important it was to prevent war since they had both experienced the agony, pain, and horror it inflicts upon humanity—unlike our baby-boomer leader who had never fought in a war.

"Besides," Zizi said, interrupting my thoughts, "we have plenty of problems right here at home that need attention. It's true that sometimes we have to stand up and fight for what is right, but we should take care of our own first and stay the hell out of other countries' business unless we're threatened. I've seen the same thing happen over and over again all my life. The deeper we get involved in another country's problems, the more it comes back to haunt us. What are we doing? Killing a lot of people for what? Remember! You reap what you sow. If we bomb them, then what's going to stop them from bombing us?"

I flashed back to 1993, when terrorists bombed the World Trade Center in New York City in retaliation for the U.S.-led Gulf War against Iraq. Strangely, despite all the media coverage of the Balkans War going on during this spring of 1999, there wasn't one single word about the possibility of retaliatory strikes against the United States for its bombing Yugoslavia. At some point, I had reasoned, as long as U.S. foreign policy continues on a trend-line of taking sides in other countries' internal conflicts, the side attacked will get even by striking back at America. Would it only be a matter of time before a new round of terrorism hit home?

"Gerald, Satan is walking the earth and getting into people. If you let the devil caress you, he'll take your soul. I think he's doing a good job at it because the bad are taking over— we're outnumbered. But I'm not afraid. I have trust in the Lord and believe in the godliness of people. If we follow the prince of light and not the prince of darkness, good will prevail over evil."

In all the years I've known Zizi, I had never heard her talk like this. Her concerns ran deep and her troubles were real. "Now they're sending our boys to Kosovo. I don't even know where it is!"

"Hardly anyone does," I said. Pick up any newspaper from March 25, 1999, the day after the bombing began, and you'll see feature stories and reports confirming that most people didn't know where the place was, or why the United States was involved. In fact, on March 7, some two weeks before the bombing began, a poll in *USA Today* showed that 75 percent of the nation did not follow international news.

Even when newspapers, such as *The New York Times*,

began covering the bombing, they ignored their own reporting, including the November 1, 1987, feature they did on the "radical nationalist" ethnic Albanians who were stealing land belonging to the Serbs, poisoning Serbian wells, burning their crops, raping Serbian girls, attacking churches, and demanding an "ethnically pure" Albanian region.

Like so many other places around the world entrenched in ethnic hatred, the cycle of violence had now merely taken another turn as the pendulum swung in the direction of the Serbs.

"I've learned in life that there are at least two sides to every story," Zizi said, "but you wouldn't know it from watching the news. No matter what channel I turn on, I always see the same faces saying the same things."

"It's all about infotainment, Zizi," I said. The media, particularly on television, had long ago stopped reporting the hard facts or details of most hard news stories. "They're so hooked on junk news that we're lucky to get even one side of a story, let alone the many sides." Actually, for over a decade the TV networks have been on a "dumb-sizing" binge. Faced with demands from Wall Street to boost their bottom line, they drastically cut their news-gathering operations, fired seasoned staff, and closed bureaus in other countries. How could we know what was going on around the world if no one was telling us? Except for a handful of big events, the share of network evening news segments devoted to international stories fell 50 percent between 1990 and 1997, according to the Center for Media and Public Affairs.

Nightline's Ted Koppel said, "People like to reduce the news to good guys and bad guys." Well, that's exactly how the war was covered: Serbs bad, Kosovar Albanians good. Just as the networks give us laugh tracks to tell us when we should laugh, they give us "mind tracks" to tell us how we should think.

"More Americans get their news from ABC than from any other source" were the final words blaring from the TV as I hit the off button on the remote. "Boy, that's a scary thought," I said to Zizi.

"Most of what they put on TV is garbage," she shot back. "I listened to the news all day yesterday, Gerald. What a bunch of shit . . . they must think we're all morons."

I scanned the kitchen table for a pencil and paper, and scribbled her exact words on the back of an envelope.

"Can I quote you, Zizi?" I asked, knowing exactly how I would contrast the hard reality of her words with her soft, beautiful face for an ad in our *Trends Journal*.

"With pleasure," Zizi replied. "And do you know what else, Jerry? These TV news people say nothing and get paid millions of dollars to say it." Zizi instructed me to "keep that damn thing off." She then said that she was becoming so disgusted with TV news that she was thinking of not watching it anymore.

Courtesy of the Trends Research Institute

The Duck-and-Cover Generation

Still sitting alone at the table, I thought about how right-on Zizi was back then, but little did I know how prophetic her words would turn out to be. In a short time, the same Albanian separatists who fought to annex Kosovo from Yugoslavia would be fighting for a slice of neighboring Macedonia.

"Are you eating?" Zizi called out from the hallway near her bedroom.

"In a minute," I replied, knowing that I couldn't yell loud enough for her to hear me at that distance.

Zizi's been around a long time and *has* seen it all before. And, as I get older, I've come to realize that I've seen quite a bit myself. When political agendas are promoted and a pliant press supports them, they are not only capable of inciting war—"Remember the *Maine*"—together they can inflict serious damage on the mental psyche.

I grew up during the Cold War when Americans were taught to hate the Russian people until they started doing *business on our terms*. I remember how we were taught not to trust those "sneaky Red Chinese," until they did *business on our terms*. As a jazz fan, I heard plenty of World War II songs written about those "dirty little Japs" and the "German vermin" before they learned how to do business *on our terms*. Who would have thought, in the heat of World War II, that after it was over America would become the largest importer of Japanese products in the world and that Germany's Deutsche Bank would seize control of Bankers Trust, and Daimler-Benz would take control of Chrysler? Make no mistake. The business of the world is business. Even Communist Vietnam, which has finally learned to do *business on our terms*, has become one of our trading partners.

As soon as Zizi entered the kitchen, slowly shuffling without the walker, I blurted out, "I got it . . . I know the answer!" as if she had been in on the thoughts swirling in my brain. "People will stop hating the Serbs once they learn how to do *business on our terms*. Yugoslavia is still an old-line socialist country."

But she either didn't hear me or chose to ignore the question. Zizi had other, more important issues to deal with. "Why aren't you eating?" she asked, seeing that the microwave was off but there was no food on the table. Without waiting for a

reply, Zizi picked up a dish towel on the counter where she had
been standing, removed the plate from the microwave, and
then slowly headed toward the utensil drawer to get me a knife
and fork.

The Cold War. Bomb shelters. The Evil Empire. I hadn't
thought of those days in many years. My mind flipped back to
Christ the King grade school and those stupid "duck-and-
cover" drills they used to run us through in the 1950s. With
air-raid sirens blaring, the nuns would make us hide under our
desks, threatening that if we spoke one word during the drill
we might wish a bomb had dropped on us. In later years, when
we grew too big to fit under the desks, they'd herd us into the
hallways and tell us to put our faces against the walls and cover
our heads with our hands. There we were, pressed up against
the wall, hands on our heads, with a phalanx of storm trooper
nuns patrolling the halls and barking out orders: "Stand up
straight! No talking! Get closer to the wall! Celente, stop
laughing!" I remember, even as a kid, thinking how funny
these drills were, instinctively knowing that if an atom bomb
dropped on us, hiding under a desk or standing in a hallway
with my hands over my head wouldn't have done a damn thing
to help save my life.

In those days you didn't question authority. You toed the
line, behaved accordingly, and did what you were told. Unfortunately for me, I joked around too much, was tagged a trou-
blemaker, and because I wasn't fitting into the mold, I'd pay a

high price. My fifth-grade teacher, the saintly Sister Marie Rosaire, drove home the message of authority when one day after prayers she marched over to where I sat at my desk, grabbed me by my little blue tie, and viciously beat me. Slapping me around like a rag doll, she severely and permanently damaged my inner ear and eardrum. My parents reacted with horror and complained to the monsignor of the parish. Mom told me I could leave and go to public school, but my older brother Anthony, whom I looked up to as a kid, said I would be a quitter if I left. So I stuck it out, and as a reward the kindly nun left me back a grade. Not only did she inflict physical damage on me, I was now looked upon as the dumbest kid in the school. In all fairness, this "bride of Christ," as nuns called themselves, did teach me a valuable lesson—wearing a tie could be hazardous to my health. To this day, I won't wear one. It serves no function other than as a handy clothing appendage for an unwelcome attacker—or wild nun—to grab hold of.

I wondered if the deranged behavior of Sister Marie Rosaire, and all the other nuns who terrorized little kids in those days, was part of a prevailing insanity that ruled the times. For example, how could an entire nation of adults have bought into the duck-and-cover stupidity? After all, they were the ones who were making us kids do these useless get-prepared-to-die drills. And it wasn't only the kids who ducked and covered—grown-ups were doing it too. Think about it. Have you ever seen photographs of a bombed Hiroshima, or the massive destructive powers of the A-bomb, as they were affectionately called? Who in their right mind would have believed that you could escape the radioactive fury of atom bombs by *covering your head with your hands*? Who? *An entire nation, that's who!* But how could they? If we believed in duck-and-cover, would that mean we're capable of believing anything that the government tells us?

It's not as though people back then were blind to what was happening—or that we were so smart and the government was so stupid. Societies often put their trust in the institutions that serve them, in good times and in bad. We believe what we are being told, with some reservation, perhaps, when it comes from certain sources. If we didn't, we'd be a bunch of paranoids.

Zizi put the steaming plate of food and utensils on the table and sat down to join me but, as usual, she didn't eat. Rather than risk a case of *acidità*, heartburn, by mixing the bitterness of world affairs with the food she had so lovingly prepared, I savored each bite of the feast set before me, and we limited our conversation to small talk.

As soon as I finished eating, Zizi said she wanted to have a cigarette. Before I could clear the table she was out on the back porch, lost in nicotine heaven. Because I really dislike breathing in cigarette smoke, and as a favor to me, Zizi said she wouldn't smoke in the house when I'm visiting her—but I've caught her red-handed a couple of times, sneaking a cigarette when she thought I was taking a nap.

"The president talked about the great victory in Kosovo," Zizi said between puffs. "So then where's the victory parade?"

"What are you talking about, Zizi?" I said as I sat in a light metal chair upwind from where she was sitting.

"The parade. Where's the ticker-tape parade to celebrate the end of the war?"

"They don't have ticker tape anymore, Zizi. Now it's just shredded paper they throw out the windows."

"Don't be so smart," she replied, smiling as she drifted backward into time. "I'll never forget the celebrations the day World War II ended. I was coming home from the hospital, August 13, 1945, after giving birth to your cousin Ronnie. He was born on August third. In those days you stayed in the hospital for ten days."

"Are you kidding, Zizi? If the health insurance companies could get away with it, they'd have drive-through delivery service. You'd be out in ten minutes—you know, like Jiffy Lube."

She chuckled at my joke, then continued. "People were pouring out of their houses and flooding into the streets. Horns were tooting and church bells were ringing. You couldn't escape the sounds of happiness or the smiles lighting up people's faces."

Even Zizi's neighbor, Mrs. Raio, who lost two sons to the war, was happy for others whose loved ones came home.

"And the parade?" I asked.

"I think every town across the country must have had victory parades, but of course nothing was like the one in New York City."

"Well, Zizi, maybe they didn't have a victory parade for Kosovo because we didn't fight a war."

"Bombs dropping, people dying—what do you call it, wise guy?" Zizi said, waving her cigarette at me with a Mae West flair.

"For someone who's so good at Scrabble, I'm shocked at your limited knowledge of the vocabulary," I teased back. "They called it the 'Conflict in Kosovo' or the 'Crisis in Kosovo.' "

"You're playing with words, Gerald. War is war. Your godfather, Uncle Albert, fought in the Philippines and was one of the few survivors of his outfit. For years he wouldn't talk about what happened. He's told me that if people really experienced the hell of war they wouldn't be so quick to start one."

"Listen, Zizi, don't pick a fight with me. You'll have to talk to our secretary of defense. When the press asked him if the United States was at war with Yugoslavia, he said, 'We're engaged in combat—whether that measures up to, quote, a classic definition of war, unquote, I'm not qualified to say.' "

"Do you mean to tell me that the secretary of defense doesn't know what a war is?" Zizi asked. "Maybe he doesn't know if he's alive!"

"You got me, Zizi. Look at Vietnam. About sixty thousand

Americans were killed, several hundred thousand seriously wounded, families ruined, and probably millions of others scarred for life, and that was never called a war. Some forty thousand Americans were killed in combat in Korea and that was a 'police action.' "

"This is why I don't trust them," Zizi said. "It's like Bill Clinton claiming oral sex isn't sex, and pretending he doesn't know what 'is' means."

"And how about this one, Zizi: 'Youthful indiscretion.' " I reminded her that that nifty little gem was coined by Congressman Henry Hyde when he was forced to admit to an extramarital affair he had carried on for several years with a married woman, when he was *forty-one years old.*

"What works for them won't work for you," Zizi replied. "The language of lies is only permitted for the kings, queens, and noblemen, not the commoners. They get to write the rule books, and you have to play by them."

Drifting back to the World War II years, Zizi reminisced about a time when there was real hope and a sense of accomplishment that all people shared. "*We* won the war. Everybody did their part," she said. "It was everybody's victory and it gave us a *can-do* feeling that we could succeed at anything we tried."

"When there was no longer work at the shipyards," Zizi continued, "your uncle Alfred went to work in a butcher shop in Mount Vernon. In the meantime, we were looking for another location for him to start his own business."

They found a store on the bottom floor of a new apartment building on Eastchester Road, in a neighborhood just a few blocks from Grandpa's house in the Bronx, where they were living. Zizi and Uncle Al needed $3,000 start-up money, but had only $1,000, so she asked her mother to loan them $1,000, and Grandma said, *"Perchè no, Filu?"* Why not, Filu (Grandma's nickname for Zizi)? My uncle Nicky loaned them the remaining $1,000.

"I remember opening day. I got all dolled up and we had a big Grand Opening party with homemade pizza and a load of treats. Right away business took off, and within two months Grandma and Uncle Nicky got their money back."

"You see, Gerald, it was blessed money. My mother and my brother Nicky gave me the money with their blessings. When you give something—money, anything—with your whole heart and soul, the person receiving it will be blessed. But if you give something against your wishes . . . even if it's a cup of coffee, it will turn sour for the giver and the taker."

Grandma's $1,000 made the rounds throughout the family. She loaned my father $1,000. Aunt Viola, Aunt Pep, Aunt Ida—it seemed like everybody was borrowing that same $1,000, paying it back, and then someone else would borrow it.

Grandma's thousand dollars, I thought to myself. That's what family life was about. "Of course, even though we all loved each other, no one is perfect and we had our share of squabbles, hurtful words, and hard feelings," Zizi said. "Life isn't perfect and neither was our family. But through thick and thin, when the chips were down, we all came together. When helping hands were needed there were always plenty to be found."

Grandma in her Bronx kitchen

The night air was turning colder, so I asked Zizi if she wanted to go back in the house.

"In a few minutes," she replied, indicating that she hadn't yet finished her smoke.

As Zizi and I reminisced about the old days, it struck me that Uncle Al had gone into business on a shoestring budget of a few thousand dollars. "Back then you didn't need to be rich,"

Zizi explained. "This really was the land of opportunity. All you needed was a dream, a few bucks, and if you were lucky, help from the family."

When Uncle Al had his butcher shop, all the shopkeepers in the area knew one another and would patronize one another's stores. There was a close-knit feeling of neighborhood and community. "When we supported our local shopkeepers, the money we spent ended up staying in the neighborhood," Zizi said.

Listening to Zizi talk about the old neighborhood reminded me of the soda fountain in the drugstore next to Uncle Al's butcher shop. They had the best lime rickeys and egg creams. Years ago, who would have thought that the trusted local pharmacist would be put out of business by giants like CVS and Eckherd? Today, less than 25 percent of the drugstores in the United States are independently owned. And, as we move into the twenty-first century, the consolidation trend will continue as multinational mega-giants devour national big boys—the killer whales will eat the barracudas.

"It was more fun to shop back then than it is today," Zizi said. "You'd go into a store from time to time just to say hello, see how they were doing, and talk about life. You'd share stories, get to know their children, and watch them grow up. In those days each neighborhood was a miniature city with a tightly knit community—the old shoemaker, the Chinese laundry, the delicatessens with their homemade specialties, the fish store, the barbershop, luncheonette, the candy store."

"Do you remember Emily's bakery?" I asked, adding to the list of neighborhood businesses. "God, I loved her pizza, what a taste!"

In those days some bakeries made pizza and Emily would make it only once a week. I can still see the little gray-haired Italian lady, always dressed in black, smiling at us kids as we'd line up at the counter, waiting for a slice of heaven. Emily would cut a big, square piece from a thick, black baking pan and hand it to us, wrapped in a piece of the white paper that bakers used. I'd savor each bite, never knowing the next time I'd get another slice of her luscious pizza.

Zizi reminded me that Aunt Ida and Uncle Albert lived in an apartment on top of Emily's on the corner of Bronxwood and Allerton avenues. In fact, the whole clan lived within a short distance of Grandma and Grandpa's house on Matthews Avenue in the Bronx.

"But you know who made the best pizza?" Zizi asked.

"Aunt Fioredeva," I answered correctly. "And let's not forget Zizi's pizza," I added.

Getting up, I extended my two arms for her to grab onto so I could lift her from her wood and canvas director's chair. "Come on, Zizi, let's go inside," I said. "It's game time."

Was Columbus in the Mafia?

"Can I get you anything? A cup of coffee? I have some nice cheesecake in the refrigerator," Zizi asked, before sitting down.

"Maybe later," I replied, and pulled the Scrabble game from the shopping bag.

The phone rang and Zizi reached up from her chair to answer it. It was Dotty, her former bingo buddy and closest friend. "One-three-three," Zizi said, as if she were speaking in code. "I can't talk now, I have a guest. My handsome boyfriend, Honeyboy, is here. I'll talk to you tomorrow," she said, and hung up the phone.

"You still playing Lotto?" I asked.

"Oh no," Zizi replied. "I told you I don't play Lotto anymore."

"Then what's this 'one-three-three' stuff about?" I asked.

"Well, that's different," Zizi quickly replied. "That was the daily number. You can't win Lotto . . . the odds are stacked against you."

Zizi likes to play the game of chance. She's as hooked on gambling as she is on cigarettes, and, like her overflowing ashtray, you can measure the extent of her betting habit by counting the multicolored lottery cards that are inevitably scattered around her kitchen.

Her favorite "scratch and win" game is Bingo. Like so many of the elderly who wait on line at the convenience store, she's short on cash, trying to make ends meet, but hopeful that Lady Luck will smile on her if she picks the right game card. Any suggestion that she's wasting her precious few extra dollars is met by a Zizi attack.

"Leave me alone!" she reprimanded when I brought up the subject. "I never go to the beauty parlor, I cut my own hair, I don't buy any clothes, I don't go to the movies, I don't go to restaurants. I don't go anyplace! So I spend a couple of dollars a week playing these games and it gives me a little enjoyment. Is that a crime?"

Playing Lotto, Take 5, Power Ball, Lucky 7, Fantasy 5, Big 3, and the long menu of state-sponsored games of chance is not a "crime." It's not a crime for states to advertise on television in order to entice lower-income people who place Lotto-type bets disproportionately, to gamble away tens of dollars per week on a game they might have a one-in-eighteen-million shot at winning. It was only a crime when these games were called "the numbers" and the states weren't getting a piece of the action. Up until the 1970s, before the government changed its moral tune and legal position, it was a serious crime for people to bet nickels and dimes to play "single," "straight," or "combination" with the bookies when the odds were only 600 to 1.

When Zizi was a young woman living in the Bronx, the old-timers who played the game relied on superstition to help them pick a set of numbers. "Suppose you had a dream about a drunken man," Zizi explained, "then the number you'd play would be fourteen. If it was Saint Anthony's feast day, you'd play thirteen. That was his number. Anything relevant to Rome meant you'd play number one. If you dreamed about a dead person, you'd play forty-eight, and so on. I don't know how they came up with these crazy things," Zizi said, "but believe me, everybody had their system and a lot of people in the neighborhood placed bets with the local bookie."

One time in the Bronx, the police busted the vegetable man, Joe, who was accused of being a numbers racketeer. Zizi remembered him as a simple, hardworking guy who was half-paralyzed and drove his old beat-up truck door-to-door selling vegetables twelve months a year in all kinds of weather. When the police arrested him you would have thought they had cracked the crime of the century. "They tied him to the mob,"

Zizi said. "So off to jail went peddler Joe." He lost his truck and his business, and his wife and kids were pushed into real hardship.

If gambling was so destructive to society back then, what makes it okay now? How does the government justify its role as bookmaker? What happened to all that moral fiber they kept feeding us, that gambling was tearing apart?

"It's like I've told you before," Zizi said with a shrug, "they write the rules and we play by them."

What James Madison had feared has become fact—the government and the politicians have elevated themselves above the citizens. Madison wrote that Congress "can make no law which will not have its full operation on themselves and their friends, as well as on the great mass of society." But that's exactly what legislators have done. Today, laws are made to meet the needs of political interests, and are bent to satisfy the agendas of special interests.

When state governments began to legalize gambling in the early 1970s, they took it out of the hands of the small-time operators, dressed it up with advertising, put it under the jurisdiction of politicians and into the hands of financiers, and then changed its name to make it proper. Now called "gaming," the once dark crime of gambling has been given the imprimatur of legality, sanitized in a cloak of corporate respectability, and protected by political muscle. Indeed, Frank Fahrenkopf, co-chair of the Commission on Presidential

Debates and former chairman of the Republican party, is president and CEO of the American Gaming Association, the trade group that represents the $40 billion casino biz.

Whether it's playing Lotto or Lucky 7 at the convenience store, playing the slots or baccarat at the casinos, or e-trading and day trading stocks on-line, a new gambling ethic has overtaken this nation's psyche. The government cons the poorest among us to bet on games we can't win. Casino operators promote big action and fast times. And like sideshow barkers, slick hypesters in three-piece suits entice us to try our luck on the stock market.

I really hit a raw nerve when I said, "Hey, Zizi, it sure was a lot easier to condemn gambling as sinful and sinister when the mob controlled it."

I could almost see the steam coming out of her ears. "All I ever heard in my lifetime was how organized crime controlled gambling and how destructive it was to society. And every time the politicians and the press talked about organized crime they'd talk about the Italians," Zizi fumed as she opened and closed her hand to mimic a flapping mouth. "Well, I'll tell you exactly where you can find the organized criminals—in Washington and on Wall Street! They crack down on the small operators while the big boys pull off deals worth billions. What a bunch of sanctimonious hypocrites." Her voice grew louder and the soft features of her face hardened.

Since coming to America, Zizi has seen prosecutors, the

police, the movies, and the media portray Italians as mobsters, crooks, killers, and *cafones*, ill-mannered, loud-talking morons. As a result, many Italian immigrants of her generation refused to allow their children to speak Italian, and they Americanized their names to fit into society.

"Let me tell you something else," Zizi said in a firm voice. "I'm sick of all this Mafia crap. I suppose Columbus was in the Mafia too! The Italians didn't corner the market on crime and we didn't invent it. It was going on long before we came to this country. Who wiped out the Indians or forced blacks into slavery? What about Baby Face Nelson, Bonnie and Clyde, John Dillinger, Jesse James, Dutch Schultz, Bugsy Siegel, and Meyer Lansky? Fine Italian boys, aren't they all?" Zizi asked sarcastically.

"Was there a Mafia? Was there organized crime? Sure, there were a few rotten apples included among the millions of Italian immigrants who came to this country, but what nationality doesn't have good and bad within it?"

I brought Zizi a recent *USA Today* front-page story, headlined DEATH OF THE MOB, which showed that organized crime—the Mafia—is virtually nonexistent in the United States; yet it's still portrayed by the media as a powerful criminal force.

This form of typecasting isn't just innocent entertainment. Vicious stereotypes breed hate and contempt. At the extremes, stereotyping can give birth to a Civil War and a Ku Klux Klan or to the Nazis and a Holocaust. At the other end of the bigotry spectrum, it fosters prejudice and condones subtle discrimination.

The Economist took an ethnic shot at Joseph Nacchio, the CEO of Qwest Communications, during his negotiations to complete a $55 billion takeover of U.S. West and Frontier. The magazine compared Mr. Nacchio, who is said to have a hot temper, to a Mafia character in the movie *Goodfellas*.

Would *The Economist* have gotten away with portraying blacks as lazy welfare queens or the Irish as drunken cops? Certainly not. When Marlon Brando said that Jews controlled Hollywood, he was condemned and had to apologize publicly for his statement. And, if *The Sopranos* brand of stereotyping is not deemed offensive by political-correctness advocates and the show is awarded trophies by the media for its "brilliance," then why not bring back *Amos and Andy*?

In 1998, I was having lunch with the chairman of a well-respected public relations firm. Over drinks he told me that he had recently moved to an exclusive enclave in Connecticut where one of his new neighbors invited him to join the country club. The neighbor said he would especially enjoy the club because there weren't any Italians. He was shocked at this gentleman's agreement—but I wasn't.

While all men are said to be created equal in America, some are treated more equally than others. Just as laws are often bent to allow the privileged and the connected to escape harsh civil penalties when they break the law, we obey a cultural law that permits racial discrimination and condones ethnic pettiness. As astonishing as it may seem, in the New Millennium overt discrimination is evidenced by the entrenched police practice of racial profiling that singles out blacks and Latinos—whether they are driving cars, walking on the street, passing through airports, going through customs, or shopping at the mall—as preselected criminals. Covertly, bigotry is still institutionalized behind closed doors.

I'm often asked about trends regarding race problems in America. I see a powder keg that is ready to explode. It will ignite when police either kill a high-profile minority leader or pump an innocent black kid full of bullets on a hot summer night. The fuse has already been lit, so it's not a matter of "if"—it's already happened.

Prejudice isn't part of Zizi's makeup. Back in the 1960s, when it wasn't generally accepted, she would warmly welcome her children's black and gay friends and classmates into her home. "We are all God's children," Zizi says, "and God created all people equal."

It was a beautiful evening, and with the back door open you could smell the sweet scents of early summer. The gently blowing breeze was just cool enough to give some relief from the heat of the day.

"I pick first, Zizi—you beat me the last time."

Believing in the
Make-Believe Ballroom

We played three games of Scrabble and didn't finish until about midnight. Finally I won one! I stayed the night and slept well. The pleasant breath of fresh, cool evening air that blew lightly through the windows of the bedroom helped dilute the heavy, stale smoke.

I woke up before Zizi, and that made me happy. She rarely sleeps more than a few hours a night and is usually up by 4:30 or 5:00 A.M. I had decided to do a little stretching and some yoga on the living room floor, when I heard Zizi yell from her bedroom, "Are you up, Gerald?"

"Yes, Zizi," I replied, "but you don't have to get up for me, sleep awhile. It's only six o'clock, I'm going to do some exercises."

"I'll be right there," she said. "I have to make you breakfast."

"No you don't," I shot back, knowing that it wouldn't matter what I said.

Within minutes, Zizi was standing at the living room entrance without her walking mate, as I began to stretch out on the thick, green carpeted floor. Wearing a long, flowing soft beige and lavender nightgown that seemed perfectly appropriate for her age and manner, she told me to keep on stretching while she made some coffee.

About fifteen minutes later, just as I was finishing up my routine, she called out, "Come and get it!"

We sat at the kitchen table at our usual places across from each other, drinking coffee and dunking her little anise cookies.

It was Friday, and I decided to take a long weekend. Today, I would be spending the morning with Zizi doing what she loves to do—being useful. Although my office hires a firm to do our large mailings, sometimes I'll take several hundred envelopes and deliver them to Zizi to stuff and seal. She really enjoys doing work because it gives her a sense of accomplishment. From time to time, I join her on the mini mail-stuffing assembly line that she sets up on her dining room table. But the work would have to wait until she attended TV mass.

Zizi watches the mass on television every morning. When

Uncle Al was alive, they would watch it together. Zizi says it's her faith in God that keeps her alive and prayer that keeps her going, "As soon as I awaken, I say good morning to the Lord and thank him for giving me another day. I pray for guidance to help me spend the day in the best way. And I ask God to please help me think what's right, do what's right, and say what's right."

When Zizi talks about God she doesn't preach or proselytize. "God is what you believe in," she tells me. "In the end all that matters is how you lived your life."

Another Zizi creed is "Don't be a taker." If you do take, give something back. She refuses to accept my financial help without doing what she can, like preparing meals when I visit and giving me a freezerload of provisions to take back home. And she despises bragging. "Grandma used to say, 'Forget the good you've done in life, only remember the bad.' Remembering the good is boasting. Remembering the bad helps you understand what you've done wrong so you can correct yourself."

The only problem I have when working with Zizi is that on whatever job she gives me to do—sealing, stuffing, collating— I'm always lagging behind her. I'm truly amazed at this elderly woman's hand speed, dexterity, coordination, agility, and work ethic. The way Zizi thinks and acts makes her seem like a young person trapped in an old person's body.

I don't attend mass, either on TV or on site, so when Zizi tuned in at 8:30 A.M., I went to buy the newspaper.

By the time I returned, mass had ended, and Zizi was setting up shop, arranging the mailing pieces on the table in the dining room that adjoins the kitchen through an archway.

Stuffing envelopes with her isn't work, it's fun. Our mission is to make jokes and laugh. And like clockwork, just a few minutes after we begin, Zizi will usually start humming a tune and then sing—word for word—an entire song. The one thing this aging swing dancer loves most is music. Sometimes I find her playing the little upright piano that sits in her living room. Years ago, after one of her daughters quit her piano lessons, Zizi taught herself how to play.

As we stuffed envelopes on this quiet morning, Zizi started humming an old tune that I remember my parents liked. They enjoyed the sounds of "The Make-Believe Ballroom" radio show; my mother's rich, husky voice singing the tunes of the day always filled our house. As a kid, my father turned me on to Dinah Washington, Peggy Lee, Xavier Cugat, and a load of old standards.

"I recognize that tune you're humming, Zizi," I said, watching her across the dining room table, busily inserting folded letters into number 10 envelopes. "But I don't know the name of it."

After a long pause, Zizi stopped what she was doing, looked up at me and in a soft voice replied, "It's 'Sonny Boy,'

Gerald. I think this is the first time I've hummed it in almost sixty years. Whenever it used to come on the radio, I turned it off because it would make me so sad. I'd call it Cosmo's song, because it would remind me of him," she said, eyes drooping downward in sorrow. "It was one of my favorites." Sweetly and mournfully, she began to sing.

SONNY BOY

When there are gray skies, I don't mind the gray skies,
    you make them blue, Sonny Boy.
Friends may forsake me, let them all forsake me,
    I still have you, Sonny Boy.
You're sent from Heaven and I know your worth
    you made a heaven for me right here on Earth.
And when the angels grow lonely they'll take you because
    they're lonely—And I'll follow you, Sonny Boy.

She sat quietly for a moment, then slowly got up and went to the corner of the dining room. Zizi isn't one to dwell on things that keep her down. She tries her best to deal with it quickly and then move on. "How about some music, Gerald? I know you like Louie Prima," she said as she pulled an LP from a well-worn record jacket and delicately placed it on the old stereo turntable. As Louie and Keely Smith belted out "That Old Black Magic," Zizi sang along with them.

"Louie Prima was great. What an entertainer, funny and talented," Zizi said, a soft smile returning to her kind, warm face. "I saw him perform live. He always would tell his band to 'play pretty for the people.' The Italians loved him and so did many of my Jewish friends. He was a character of the times and he had a gift for bringing out the good warm feelings in people."

Zizi sat back down at the dining room table and went back to work, but she was off in another world and in another time zone, the 1930s. "The Depression was tough for a lot of people, but it was a great time for the hottest, happiest music this country has ever known," she said. "I had the time of my life growing up during the Swing Era."

As the music of Louie Prima continued to play in the background, Zizi told me that during the Depression she had the good fortune to land a decent job. After graduating from Bird's Business School on 149th Street and Melrose Avenue in the Bronx, she went to work with her two cousins, Angie and Margaret, at Gotham Gold Stripe, a hosiery company on Thirty-third Street and First Avenue in Manhattan.

"The boss, Mr. Jacobson, told me there were no openings for office work," Zizi told me, "but there was a job for examining silk stockings. So I gave it a try. Being that it was piecework, the more you examined, the more money you could earn. I was really fast with my hands so I was earning thirty-five dollars per week. And that was good money back then."

"So now I know why you're such a fast envelope stuffer and paper collator! You've had years of experience," I said.

Zizi replied with a wink and smile, and continued to tell me about the old days. After about two or three months, Mr. Jacobson called her down to his office and said he had a clerical opening. The pay was $12 a week. "I told him no thanks, I'd rather stay upstairs inspecting stockings," she said. "I asked Mr. Jacobson if he'd mind, and he said, 'It's all right. We know you're a hard worker and we like you, Phyllis.' "

Zizi was popular and the people in her department elected her union representative. With the Depression going on and good jobs scarce, you would think that people would have been afraid of getting fired if they organized or went out on strike, but the opposite was true. By sticking together, workers gained *more* rights, and the brotherhood and sisterhood of unions grew stronger. "When I started working in 1932, our hours were from 8:30 A.M. to 6:00 P.M., with a half-hour lunch. But after Franklin Roosevelt became president, we worked nine to five here with an hour lunch."

When Zizi gave me the next photo she also showed me a pair of Gotham Gold Stripe silk stockings that she still has. Taking them from their original box, she expertly refolded the stockings to show me how she did it back in the 1930s when she was on the job. "I had pride in my work," she said, beaming, "and so did everyone else. We were so thankful to have good jobs and the owners of Gold Stripe appreciated how hard we worked," Zizi said.

Zizi at Gotham's Christmas celebration in 1933

As I scanned the photo trying to find her, it struck me how beautifully dressed everyone was and how happy they looked. And even though it was the height of the Great Depression, the workers were treated to a gala Christmas celebration. How times have changed. Blue-collar and service workers don't even get a holiday turkey anymore.

One reason Zizi got to see so many live band performances was that she had a daily routine. She made it her business to do enough piecework so that she could make $7 by noontime. "If a big-name band or entertainer was in town, I'd just take off the rest of the afternoon and go to the show," she recalled.

The movies would start about one o'clock in the afternoon, and then after the movie came the stage show. She saw all the greats—Jimmy Durante, Ethel Merman, Cab Calloway, Eddie Duchin, Louis Armstrong, Vincent Lopez, Count Basie, Glenn Miller, Benny Goodman, Harry James, Lanny Ross, Bob Eberly, Helen O'Connell, Jimmy and Tommy Dorsey, Duke Ellington, Guy Lombardo, Artie Shaw, Glen Gray, Bunny Berrigan, Spike Jones, Sammy Kaye, Kay Kyser, the Andrews Sisters. "Oh, how I loved the way Paul Whiteman played 'Rhapsody in Blue.' I even took Grandma to see Rudy Vallee at the Loews State." Pausing for just a moment, Zizi recalled that the accompanying movie that night was *Rosalie* with Jeanette MacDonald and Nelson Eddy.

"The stage shows at the Paramount were magnificent," she said, beaming. "After the movie ended, you'd then hear the sounds of an orchestra or big band playing. But the stage was empty. The music would get a bit louder and, very slowly, the orchestra would begin to appear, as they were elevated up from below the stage. And, oh, how the audience would applaud! It was really a thrill. The band would play a few popular tunes before a young man tap-danced. Then the big act would come out and the place would go wild."

Zizi was off and flying as she relived an era and emotion of a time long past. As she talked, I jumped on board her trip, feeling as though I were sitting in the balcony of the Paramount, imagining the styles and hearing the sounds she was describing. With her hand resting on her chin, and her beautiful hazel eyes lost in space, Zizi played back one of the many stage performances she saw at the Paramount.

"The theater was dark except for one spotlight brightly shining on the curtain on the right side of the stage. With the music softly playing in the background, I remember how gracefully George Raft came out from behind it. There he was, this dashing figure, elegantly dressed, standing in the spotlight with a cigarette in his mouth. Without saying a word or making a motion to acknowledge the applause, he took the cigarette from his mouth, tossed it on the floor, and with a twisting motion of his foot, he put it out. And then . . . flash! Another spotlight beamed onto the curtain at the opposite end of the stage. The music grew just a little louder. Out from behind that curtain slinked a beautiful blonde—a Carole Lombard type. The music built as the blonde and George Raft glided from their corners toward the center of the stage. Just as the music hit full tempo, their outstretched hands joined and they lightly embraced. Pausing for just a moment, they looked at each other like two lovers who had just been reunited, and then they began to dance the bolero."

Back then, a movie and stage show cost 50 cents. Zizi got to see many of the greatest names in twentieth-century entertainment for under a dollar. Then, after the show, she and her friends would go to Chin Lee's Chinese restaurant, and for 90 cents eat dinner, listen to a band, and dance. "I have to tell you, it was really a time for happy feet!" she said.

Zizi and her cousins would go dancing every week before she got married. She told me that she would never dance with a short man, even though they were often the best dancers. And then, as life would have it, she married a short guy with two left feet. "When your uncle Al and I would dance, I'd lead," Zizi said with a little smile, "but I'd make it look like he was." Zizi said that she felt sorry for me and the younger generations that missed out on the sounds and styles of a time when people were "putting on the Ritz." She even remembers when they built Radio City Music Hall.

"I don't think Limp Bizkit could compare to Louis Armstrong," I said as Zizi evoked the Golden Era of music.

"What the hell does a limp biscuit have to do with Louis Armstrong?" Zizi asked.

"Not a damn thing, Zizi. Forget it—they're just talentless kids with an attitude who have next to nothing to do with music."

I reminded her not to forget that there was some great music in my youth, too, and the sensations that Elvis, The Beatles, Motown, and others created over the last fifty years. I told Zizi that while there was a lot of great music back in her day, there was also some dreadful stuff like that "Lambsey oats and dotsey dotes" song.

"It's not 'lambsey oats.' It's 'mareseatoats and doeseatoats and little lambseativy,'" Zizi interjected with a song in her voice. "Oh, I almost forgot. I saw Sinatra many times. The last time was May of 1977 when he performed at the Westchester Premier Theater with Dean Martin."

Zizi says she liked Sinatra but *loved* Dean Martin. So she decided to arrange a beautiful basket of roses to give Dino. "With the condition of my legs, it was too hard for me to walk up to the stage to give Dean the flowers so I put the arrangement in your uncle's arms and sent him up to the stage," Zizi said as a million-dollar smile filled her face.

As Uncle Al walked down the side aisle, Dean Martin spotted him, stopped the show, and said, "Hey, champ, what've you got there?" Uncle Al said, "My wife made this floral arrangement for you." Dean walked over to meet Al, took the flowers from him, and said, "Your wife made these for me? How beautiful!" Then he held the basket up for everyone to see and the audience applauded. Frank Sinatra got into the act and complained that Dean got roses and he didn't get anything. Zizi was so thrilled.

I asked Zizi to tell me the first thing that came to her mind when comparing the music, musicians, and singers of her day to those of today. Without giving the question a second thought, she said, "In one word, refined. The ladies looked and acted like ladies and the men dressed and acted like men. They were dignified."

"Dignified." Instantly I thought of one face and one voice when I heard that word. It was spoken by my dear friend John when he described the people in an old photograph that hangs over the credenza in my office. Considering the photo he was

looking at, I thought his interest in it seemed a bit odd. Young, avant-garde, and hip, John usually showed no feeling for the sounds or styles of the past.

"Look at them, and you'll see the big difference between people back then compared to now," John said as he stood alone, staring at a picture that he had overlooked so many times before.

At age thirty, John had a commanding presence, and when he talked, you *had* to listen. If you didn't give him your undivided attention, he'd give you his mock cold stare and a half-smile sneer. Standing erect, yet relaxed, he dissected each element of the image and the people in it. "Look at the expressions on their faces, their posture, their clothes. These people were dignified," John commented as he picked apart each person in the photo, which was taken on January 28, 1934. The place was New York City. The event was my parents' wedding.

Dignified they were. Although they looked like members of the uptown elite, each person in the photo was a first-generation immigrant from a family of modest means. And while they were dressed for a first-class affair, my parents' bash was called a "football" wedding because the families of the bride and groom had rented a large wedding hall and filled a table the size of a football field with a variety of Italian foods, wine, and pastries.

Zizi had designed the dresses for the wedding party, including my mother's wedding gown, which was hand-sewn by Grandma. The bridesmaids wore sky blue with silver accessories and silver shoes, while Zizi, my mother's maid of honor, wore a silver lamé gown with sky-blue accessories and shoes.

My parents and their wedding party; Zizi as maid of honor

As if someone had dropped a nickel in the jukebox slot, Zizi began singing one of her old favorites, interrupting my reverie:

FORGIVE ME

Forgive me, please forgive me, I didn't mean to make you
   cry,

I love you and I need you, say anything but don't say
   good-bye.
Let bygones just be bygones, we all make mistakes now
   and then,
I'm sorry, forgive me my dear, and let's be sweethearts
   again.

"Any other songs you want me to sing?" Zizi said with a girlish smile. Lost in my thoughts, I didn't respond. The memories I was reliving had turned bittersweet. Seeing that I was troubled, Zizi asked what was wrong. "I was thinking about what happened to John," I replied.

When the Angel Passes
and Says Amen

For about ten years I was a member of the John, Jesse, and Jerry trio—three inseparable friends who hung out together, flew around in Jesse's hot-air balloon, and dreamed up wild adventures to go on. We met in the early 1980s at a party in Woodstock, New York, where Jesse and John both lived. They were single, the outdoors type, and had a world of interests in common. And although I was married and lived about thirty minutes away on the other side of the Hudson River, I was in the mix.

John worked with me for a while, and we frequently went on business trips together. He had many attributes I wished I had, particularly his elegance, sleek style, and sensitivity to those less fortunate than himself. If a friend needed a favor,

John would always be there. When the chips were down, you always could count on him.

But by the early 1990s our paths began to split as we moved in different directions with our lives and interests. Jesse had gotten married and he was devoting his time to his booming tree-removal business and new family. I was on the road more and had less time to socialize. And John went off on his own, determined to turn a musical spin wheel he invented into a business success. Mounted on a stick, just like the spin wheels children play with, the spinning wheel would play a tune, such as "Happy Birthday" or "When Irish Eyes Are Smiling." John believed that they would make great little gifts for a variety of holidays.

In the fall of 1993, after John returned home from a year spent traveling between California and China, he was a different person. His business venture had failed and he was deeply in debt and had become a trembling wreck. Also down on his romantic luck, he was depressed about a freshly failed relationship.

One day John stopped by to talk, but I was late for a meetting and in a hurry. We chatted a bit before I ran off. As I drove away, the image of John haunted me. He looked like hell. Worried about his condition, I telephoned Jesse later that evening and said, "John is really in bad shape. I'm afraid he's going to kill himself." After talking with Jesse, I called John. I was leaving for a business trip in a few days and made plans to see him when I returned.

I called Jesse back and we talked about what to do, but in the end neither of us did enough. When John called out for help and was sinking in desperation, no one was there to throw him a rescue line of love, or a life preserver of compassion. We were busily wrapped up in our own lives and increasingly unwilling to deal with his growing problems. We rationalized that because John was strong-willed he probably wouldn't listen to anyone, and that he was capable of taking care of himself.

Just one week later, on December 9, 1994, John shot himself through the heart in front of his ex-girlfriend on a street in Rhinebeck. The common disclaimer that came from friends, acquaintances, and the shrinks was, "When someone is going to commit suicide there's nothing you can do to stop it. So don't feel guilty. You did your best."

No I didn't. I knew how desperate John was and so did everyone else who knew and loved him. But I can honestly say that not one of his friends or loved ones did enough. We put a priority on our time above his needs. When the chips were down for John, we weren't there for *him*. I'm convinced that had we done more, John would have weathered the emotional storm.

After John's death I poured my heart out to Zizi about how, as a friend, I failed him. Not the type to judge, Zizi would mostly listen, but I'll never forget what she told me. Quoting Byron, she said: " 'The dew of compassion is a tear,' "

I began to understand that the tears I shed were not only

for his loss, but also for my lack of true compassion. I was deeply aware not only of John's suffering, but also my failure to help. "No one is perfect. Learn from your mistakes," Zizi would tell me.

Promising myself that I wouldn't make the same mistake twice, I was given the opportunity to keep to my word, when my good friend Stuart came to me for support when he was teetering on the edge of emotional despair.

Stuart and I met in the early 1980s while we practiced martial arts at the same dojo. In later years he and I would team up to run our own school for close-combat self-defense. Stuart was born and raised in the hardscrabble South Bronx ghetto. Besides being poor, he lost his parents when he was a young boy. Still, he did his best to lift himself out of the slum world he came from and into a better life.

Evolving from a grunt in the Marines, he started his own chimney-sweep business—a grimy job he grew to hate, but diligently performed so he could earn a decent living. In a visionary leap that was guided by his ravenous appetite for reading and his hard-knocks common sense, Stuart sensed, in the mid-1980s, that the alternative health field could provide him with some promising opportunities. By literally scraping together nickels and dimes and living on a shoestring, Stuart became one of New York State's first licensed acupuncturists.

But Stuart has two big strikes against him. Strike one: he doesn't have great marketing skills. Strike two: Stuart's "sin" is in the color of his skin. A lot of white folks don't feel comfortable having a six-foot-four-inch black man sticking needles in them. A few acquaintances in the medical field told me they would like to use Stuart, but didn't feel their white upscale clientele would accept him. These guys aren't racists, that's just the way it is.

Out of work and convinced that his future held no promise, Stuart sank into depression and spoke desperate thoughts. As I saw this happen, I thought about John and how much I missed him and what a waste it was that he was no longer on earth to share life with me.

I told Stuart how I truly loved him like a brother. I told him to call me whenever he needed me—day or night, at home or at work—and I made him promise that he would. I'd regularly call him to check in to see how he was doing.

"Guess what, Zizi?"

Breaking the silence of my thoughts, I gave Zizi some good news about Stuart. He had persevered, was now knee-deep in work as an acupuncturist, and had paid the check at our recent dinner with his new platinum Visa card.

"God bless Stuart," Zizi said in response to his good fortune.

Zizi said that John's loss is a terrible tragedy, and that Stuart's success is a reminder of how desperately we all crave compassion and how little of it we each bestow upon our fellowman.

"So many people are starving for love and understanding,"

I said to Zizi, sharing the memory of John that lives so strong within me.

"Yes," she said, "maybe it all boils down to one person helping one person."

After my experiences with John and Stuart, and knowing that there are millions of others suffering through hard times without a helping hand, I was compelled to make my company's mission statement one of compassion—a trend that I believe will be a cornerstone in building the foundation of New Millennium thinking. As the Industrial Age dies, its survival-of-the-fittest philosophy will be replaced by a Global Age school of thought, one in which dogs *don't* eat dogs, and compassion, cooperation, and interdependency dominate. To help make our trend come true, and in celebration of the next millennium, I commissioned a painting, entitled "Compassion," by the French-born artist Marie-Pierre Astier. Her work had been exhibited at the Cathedral of Saint John the Divine in New York, and I was taken by her unique ability to blend the quality and essence of Renaissance art with a futuristic vision.

Zizi kept working away as I was talking about my millennium hopes, but her mind and body seemed to be in two different places, because the motions she made putting letters into envelopes seemed entirely mechanical. "Actions speak louder than words," Zizi said suddenly as a serious expression overtook her face. "Sometimes we are so trapped in our small worlds and so self-absorbed in our little minds that we neglect what's really important in life. You show compassion and love by giving of yourself and not by just talking about it. To love is the greatest gift that God gave us and is the greatest gift we can give to God."

"Compassion"

I never told John that I loved him, but I never get off the telephone without saying "I love you" to Stuart. At one time it was awkward for me to say this to another guy, but I became more comfortable after hearing a legendary college basketball coach speak at a conference I was attending at the Broadmoor Hotel in Colorado. I had just delivered a talk and was preparing to leave when the organizer of the meeting encouraged me to stay for the next speaker. "You have to hear this guy," he said. "You'll make a mistake if you leave."

The speaker was the now departed Jim Valvano of North Carolina State fame. To say the least, Valvano had a real loose style and was a great showman. He talked about his basketball coaching career, his childhood upbringing, and his family life. There were no slides or glitzy graphics. It was just Valvano and his captivated audience. Hearing him talk about his loving wife, close-knit family, and his professional successes made me say to myself, "Good for you, Jim. You did it right." Throughout his talk, he told stories about his father and how very close they were. One of the things his father taught him was how important it was to say "I love you" when saying good-bye to a loved one, whether in person or on the telephone—even if you've had an argument with that person—because you never know if it will be your last good-bye. As only Valvano could have done, he brilliantly wove this message into the climax of his talk. He told us of his last good-bye to his father, who died suddenly, and how happy he was that the last words they exchanged with each other were "I love you."

"I'll be right back," Zizi said, pushing herself up from the chair. It seemed to take every ounce of strength she had to lift her aging, arthritic body. "I want to show you something that I have in my bedroom," she said as she brushed her walker aside and speed-shuffled across the floor.

"Hey, no breaks allowed," I teased. "You'll set a bad example for the rest of the workers." As she reached my chair, Zizi stopped for a few seconds, gave me a warm smile, stroked my head, and kissed me on the cheek before she resumed her journey.

Zizi moved at a pretty good clip. I wondered if stuffing envelopes and having a sense of purpose had anything to do with her ability to walk quicker and without the walker.

It took only a few minutes for her to return to the dining room clutching a small black leather book. Lowering herself back into her chair, she pushed the book across the table toward me. "Turn to any page," she instructed, "it's all the same." As I flipped from page to page, I began to get the message. It was Zizi's address book. Virtually every name and address had been crossed out.

"Practically everyone is gone," Zizi said. "Most of my friends and family are dead . . . it's hard to believe. And soon I'll be gone, but I'm not quite ready."

When I gave it back to her, she said, "One of the saddest things about getting old is being without those you love. Cherish the treasures of friendship and always remember that John was a rare blessing."

It's not only her friends who have passed on. The world Zizi was born into is also gone forever. She arrived at a unique time in civilization. Her generation was the last to have left a footprint in the Old World, with ties to ancient customs, traditions and beliefs. Despite two millennia of dramatic changes, traces of the old ways could still be recognized in the world into which Zizi had been born. When she was a little girl, living in her native Italy, the people there—and even those in the most developed countries—still followed a lifestyle recognizably based upon the past. Without electricity or modern machines, the farmers worked the land pretty much the way they had back in medieval times. Cooking was done in wood-fired ovens. People still traveled around by horse and buggy. Just think: from Julius Caesar to Grover Cleveland, world leaders all rode to their coronations and inaugurations in horse-drawn vehicles.

In Zizi's day, religious doctrine still ruled supreme. Families and communities were tightly knit, and the extended family unit—three generations living in one household—was still intact. In Zizi's day, a woman's job meant raising a family, keeping house, and cooking meals from scratch. Only the rich had housekeepers, telephones, and automobiles—or could afford to go on vacations. It wasn't until Zizi was a young adult that people had radios, and it would be many years later before television became a household staple. There were no refrigerators. For 10 cents you'd get a big block of ice to keep your food cold; Zizi told me that it was her job to empty the pan at the bottom of the icebox and throw out the water that dripped from the melted ice.

"So here we are, Zizi, at the dawn of the New Millennium," I said. "We can't bring the past into the future, or transfer the values and ideas of an age that nourished your soul and enriched your spirit."

"Not so fast," she replied as she finished collating the mail. "There is a lot about the past that can be brought forward."

"Like what?" I asked, hoping for a silver bullet.

"Caring and kindness. People had a lot less money back when I was young and growing up, but they gave a lot more of themselves to others. That doesn't have to die . . . it can be part of your new world. People must practice how to give a helping hand before we come to the Day of Reckoning."

It's the mind—not the machine—that will ultimately determine the quality of New Millennium life. It's our thoughts and actions that will shape the future. Individually and collectively, how we feel and how we think dominate our personal actions and shape our planet's destiny. If we take actions toward being more respectful toward ourselves, other people, animals, or trees—all living things—then that will be our destiny. If we understand that we're not the only ones whose every need must be satisfied and that a whole world lives around us, we could better understand the need for more balance, beauty, and harmony.

Uncle Mario, Aunt Rose, Uncle Dominick, Aunt Grace, Uncle Alfred, Uncle Nicky, Aunt Viola, Aunt Pep, Uncle Frankie, Uncle Albert, the Singers, Harold and Herbie, John, Louie, and Marie . . . these are just a few of the family and friends who are gone but not forgotten. None of them were perfect but, to a person, each one of them was *kind, gentle, and generous.* That's who they were, that's what I cherish about them, and it's this part of their legacy that I want to try my best to keep alive and put into practice for the rest of my life.

"We shouldn't underestimate ourselves," Zizi counseled. "You see, it's how we think and what we think that will bring us either shades of brightness or hues of gray. When I was a little girl, Grandma would tell me that departed spirits or

"The Emperor Angel"

angels watch over us. Sometimes, when I was complaining about something unimportant or being unappreciative, Grandma would say, *'Quanda passe angela e dice amen,'* When the angel passes and says amen. It was her way of telling me that if I wanted to be miserable, the angel would grant my wish when it passed over me and said amen, so be it.

"Grandma taught me to think of brightness, hope, compassion, and love. We can't afford to dwell on negative thoughts, Gerald. You may think I'm just a crazy old lady, but I know that the world can be a better place. . . . I think the people who *don't* think it can be better are the crazy ones! We must put our trust in the power and glory of the God within us. We need to have faith in ourselves. *Quanda passe angela e dice amen.*"

We finished our stuffing job by lunchtime, and somehow I managed to convince Zizi not to feed me. I made a few trips to the car with the bins of mail and two of Zizi's care packages. After I loaded up, I went back into the house to say good-bye and get some loving kisses and squeezes of affection.

"Oh, Gerald, you made my day," Zizi said as she escorted me to the front door. "When will I see you again?"

I gave her another hug and a kiss and said, "You know me, Zizi, it could be next week or tomorrow. I'll see you the next time I have to go to the city. I love you."

Just as I reached my car, Zizi called out, "Honeyboy?"

Standing at the front door, with one hand grasping the half-opened screen door for balance, she waved to me with the other and said, "*Cresce santo figlio mio*, Grow like a saint, my son."

I waved back and said, "I'll do my best, Zizi."

"Amen," she replied.

It's Your Move

Something precious has been lost. Something troubles us. It is in the air, and although we can't see it, we feel it deep inside. While it is true that progress has brought us many creature comforts that have enhanced our lifestyles, has the quality of our lives really improved? Is the progress we've achieved more important than the values we've left behind?

Zizi's not one to turn her back on the better things in life. And like other folks, she worries about her health and having enough money to pay the bills. But she's more a part of America's past than present. Her life is centered on kindness, love of God, singing old songs, praying for the living and the dead, having a good laugh, and playing Scrabble. I can't count the times I've heard her say to me after a visit, "You've made my day." Seeing how little it takes to make her happy helps me to be grateful for all I have and reminds me to resist the myth that more money and material possessions will bring me more joy and satisfaction.

Feeling rejected, lost, and alone in the world, I was fortunate to have Zizi to lean on when I was suffering through my divorce. Without her, there would have been no one to remind me of my heritage and instill within me the self-esteem and sense of pride that comes from being a member of a family with its own identity, culture, and traditions. "Remember, you come from good stock," Zizi would tell me. "Your great-grandmother was educated, a *signora*, a lady; she knew how to read and write," she'd say to illustrate that my roots were solid and that my parents and relatives were good people who did their best to teach me well.

While Zizi's an original, she's also a symbol of our nation's melting-pot values and elder wisdom. But in America's obsession to embrace a youth culture, we have lost contact with her generation's most precious memories and cherished values, as well as our social history. Always searching for the next big thing, we have forgotten the treasures that we already have: the wisdom of our elders and all that they have to offer.

Find your Zizi before it's too late. The men and women of her era won't be around much longer. Make time to visit your grandparents whom you hardly see anymore because you are too busy. Reconnect with that Aunt Pearl or Uncle Frank who treated you special when you where a kid, but for whatever reasons you've drifted apart. Give a call or drop in to say hello to the Mr. Smith or Mrs. Jones who have touched your life with words of wisdom and generous warmth. And how about the old Tom, Dick, or Mary who live across the street or down the hall whom you bump into from time to time and who have a twinkle in their eye and kindly ways that tell you that they're someone you should get to know. Pay attention to what they tell you, and try to give them what you can. For every ounce of love you show, the helping hand you extend, the companionship you share, or even the bit of cash you might offer, you will get back enough interest, knowledge, and principle to make you feel like the richest person in the world.

Acknowledgments

In the world of publishing Joann Davis stands out for her insights, sensitivity, intuition, and kindness. I'm the fortunate guy to have such a wonderful person as both my very dear friend and agent. In my twenty-five-year career, I have never worked with a more intelligent and caring team of gentlemen and gentlewomen than those assembled by Michael Morrison, publisher of William Morrow and Company. Mauro DiPreta, the executive editor stands out for his hard work and dedication in guiding me to continually fine-tune this book to make it the best it could be. He went above and beyond the call of duty. My special thanks to Joelle Yudin, Mauro's assistant, for keeping things on track and for her observations and suggestions. I am most grateful to Judy O'Neill, my trusted assistant, whose bright disposition, smiling face, and warm heart truly reflects the purpose of the Trends Research Institute—to create products and services for the betterment of life.

About the Author

Gerald Celente founded the Trends Research Institute in Rhinebeck, New York, in 1980. He is publisher of *The Trends Journal*, a quarterly newsletter that is distributed to businesses and media worldwide, and the author of *Trends 2000*.

With over twenty years' experience and a documented record of predicting future trends from current events, Gerald Celente appears regularly in the national media and is a sought-after speaker on the business circuit. He is a frequent guest on the CNN network and has appeared on *Oprah*, ABC, CBS, MSNBC, FOX, CNBC, and PBS, as well as in a variety of national print publications and radio programs.

For information about the Trends Research Institute and *The Trends Journal*, call 1-800-25-Trend or visit www.trends research.com.